Conflict and a Christian Life

Conflict and a Christian Life

Sam Portaro

MOREHOUSE PUBLISHING
HARRISBURG, PENNSYLVANIA

Morehouse Publishing

Editorial Office:
871 Ethan Allen Hwy.
Ridgefield, CT 06877

Corporate Office:
P.O. Box 1321
Harrisburg, PA 17105

Library of Congress Cataloging-in-Publication Data
Portaro, Sam Anthony.
    Conflict and a Christian Life / Sam Portaro.
        p.   cm.
    ISBN 0-8192-1653-4 (pbk.)
    1. Conflict management—Religious aspects—Christianity.
    2. Conflict management in the Bible.   I. Title.
    BV4597.53.C58P67   1996
    248—dc20   95-49873
                                                            CIP

Printed in the United States of America

Cover art: *Jacob Wrestling with the Angel*, Odilon Redon,
        Lerner/Superstock.

Contents

o John

Acknowledgments

This book owes its genesis to the people of the Church of the Holy Spirit in Lake Forest, Illinois, who first invited me to address a Sunday morning adult forum on the role of conflict in a Christian life. Mr. Rhett Butler, who was present on that occasion, brought my perspectives to the attention of Allen Kelley, who invited me to work with Morehouse Publishing to expand my initial remarks. Deborah Grahame-Smith's fine editorial skills helped bring the project to fruition.

In addition to many years of warm friendship, Paul Welbon, and his late wife, Norma, provided an introduction to Jane Blaffer Owen, whose generous hospitality at New Harmony, Indiana, offered the perfect blend of quiet celebration and restful reflection appropriate to the completion of the first draft. While visiting there, I was also introduced to words of Thomas Merton appropriate to begin this venture:

> As long as we are on earth, the love that unites us will bring us suffering by our very contact with one another because this love is the resetting of a body of broken bones—even saints cannot live with saints on this earth without some anguish. Without some pain at the differences that come between them. There are two things men can do about the pain of disunion with other men—they can love or they can hate. (*Seeds of Contemplation*)

I am profoundly grateful for the sacrifices of all those persons in my life, and our world, who choose love over hate.

Thanksgiving Day, 1995

Turn thou us, O good Lord, and so shall we be turned. Be favourable, O Lord, Be favourable to thy people, Who turn to thee in weeping, fasting, and praying. For thou art a merciful God, Full of compassion, Long-suffering, and of great pity. Thou sparest when we deserve punishment, And in thy wrath thinkest upon mercy. Spare thy people, good Lord, spare them, And let not thine heritage be brought to confusion. Hear us, O Lord, for thy mercy is great, And after the multitude of thy mercies look upon us; Through Jesus Christ our Lord. Amen.

The Book of Common Prayer (1928), p. 62

Introduction

SOME YEARS AGO I visited the small, remote village of Malvagna in Sicily, from which my father's family originated. The people there were unaccustomed to strange visitors and greeted them with obvious suspicion. Not knowing the language or the customs, I was equally uncomfortable with their strangeness and the sidelong glances that followed me when I walked alone in the streets. The tension was eased by relatives. In their presence, I was accepted by the villagers because of my relationship with people they knew. Similarly, in the presence of relatives, I was reassured that I had a legitimate relationship with those strangers. But without those obvious and established relationships, both I and the villagers were afraid.

My strangeness and the difference of the Sicilian villagers came together in our daily meeting. Fortunately, our differences never collided, so actual conflict never marred my visit. But they and I were always cautious, careful lest our differences come against each other too hard. And even though I knew ease and love in the presence of mediating family, I also knew that I was never far from potential conflict.

Yet conflict can actually be a force for good. Conflict is a necessary element of the created order by which all life is sustained. Therefore conflict is not just a problem to be resolved. Indeed, some conflict may not be resolvable. Some differences cannot easily or readily be reconciled. Some questions and issues will continue to defy even our best attempts to come to decision or determination. The challenge of such conflicts suggests that even as we work for resolution, we need some hopeful and helpful understanding of the role of conflict.

The word *conflict* means, literally, "to strike together." Conflict is the collision of differences. The confrontation of difference may be ordered and civil, or it may be chaotic and violent. It is always challenging and often painful. We are largely averse to pain, so we instinctively shy from that which is potentially painful.

1

And we are instinctively fearful of anything that threatens us. Our instinct for survival predisposes us to respond defensively, to turn away from anything that could alter the way we are. So we are fearful of difference, in part, because our own sense of self is so poorly or tentatively defined. We are not always confident of our own strength or of our boundaries. We are not always sure of ourselves, of who we are, and what our place in the world is to be.

We are more and more aware of difference and of change. While it may be true that we live in a time of unusually rapid change, the rate of change may not be as rapid as the rate of growing awareness. Negotiating who we are as individuals, and how we are to be in relationship with others, is some of the hardest work we do in our lives. Increasingly, we are asked to do more of this work, and we are asked to do it more quickly.

As I was reminded by my sojourn in Sicily, human relationships take time—time to begin and time to mature. The processes by which a relationship is built and sustained are not nearly so rapid as the technologies that now connect us. These technologies encourage in us a growing impatience about our own limitations, including our inability to process the many potential relationships offered in modern society or to negotiate our sense of self within them.

The combined sensations of familiarity and fear that marked my time in Sicily also describe the way I experience life in society and in the church. For society and church too are embroiled in conflict.

Increasingly, we face the realities of the genuine and growing differences among us. The backlog of unresolved conflict grows, despite our attempts to order and control it with politeness. Our civility is strained to the breaking point. Sadly, but remarkably, our most expressive moments of unity are motivated by tragedy, and those tragedies are frequently the result of explosive anger ignited by unresolved conflict. We lament the loss of community when what we really grieve is our growing sense of how little we hold in common, and the isolation, loneliness, and fear this awareness engenders. We are especially fearful because the customary devices of law that order our life together will not avail.

For instance, this became quite evident in the House of Bishops at the 1991 General Convention of the Episcopal Church when deliberations on proposed legislation on sexuality and ordination became so volatile that the Presiding Bishop moved the House to "executive session," thus keeping this rancorous display from public exposure.

The disagreements that flared up and boiled over were not entirely resolved, but from that occasion onward, the bishops determined that a new way of negotiating their differences was needed. They recognized that avoidance was neither helpful nor a healthful way to proceed. But neither was open warfare. The bishops sought and eventually found a way to carry on their conversations with mutual respect for each person's difference. Conflict can and will continue to be present in the deliberations of the bishops and of their congregations and communicants. But conflict need not be destructive. In this instance, at least, it served to turn the bishops from contention to conversation, a step toward community and communion.

The experience of the bishops is illustrative of the more common experience of the modern church member. It is also the more prominent image of the church in the public sphere, where bad news seems always to supersede good news. The evangelical proclamation of God's good news is too often obscured by debate and controversy. Joyful thanksgiving for God's abundant love is too frequently overshadowed by anxiety over how bad things are and how much worse they are getting. Despite—or even alongside—the rich and happy experiences of Christians in many places, one must also acknowledge and accept that many other Christians are divided and depressed, angry and arguing.

Are we to read and accept the Bible literally and uncritically, or not? Should women be ordained, or not? Do the formal language and images of our liturgies exclude some people, or not? Is there a place for baptized gay men and lesbian women in the full life of the church, or not? Are we racist, or not? Shall we engage in political action, or not? Are we too much influenced by our times and culture, or too little? Are our institutional and administrative structures hierarchical and exclusive, or not?

3

Can we resolve our differences, or not? This question emerges as one of the most pressing. There is concern that continuing in conflict will inevitably destroy us; our weariness with nearly three decades of intense debate only heightens this worry. Some maintain that we have already gone too far, that our differences have already damaged the church beyond repair.

Our questions are passionate and so is our concern. Yet the passions generated by conflict, no matter how wide their range, are also expressions of fear. And fear is the antithesis, the opponent, of faith.

When Jesus revealed himself to his disciples after the Resurrection, his appearing in their midst was itself a conflict. Separated by the experiences of death and resurrection, Jesus and the disciples were profoundly different. Whenever they came together there was a fearful meeting of differences, a "striking together" —a head-on collision of differences. On many of those occasions Jesus' first words to them were, "Do not be afraid."

Jesus was not responding to their doubt, but to their fear. Coming to grips with our fear is not an easy thing. Yet even the suggestion that fear is the basis of our responses to differences can put us on the defensive, redoubling our denial and escalating our emotions.

Rather than face the fear at the heart of conflict, we avoid by whatever means possible the painful work of resolution. Arriving at genuine resolution entails the difficult matter of engaging differences honestly, usually with the help of a mediator, an objective outsider whose skillful listening and direction can help us through our fears. But the process of resolution is seldom easy.

A medical analogy may be helpful in describing the process. As a teenager I landed in a hospital emergency room in the wee hours of the morning with a problem very obvious to me, but not so obvious to an observer. Pain was coursing through my body and growing more intense by the moment. Despite my agony, none of the attending personnel would give me even a mild pain killer. My doctor had been called, they explained, and when he arrived he would need to know exactly where I was hurting in order to know exactly what was wrong with me.

When my doctor finally arrived and began touching my body in various places, I had very little difficulty telling him exactly what was hurting, how it was hurting, and where it was hurting. Once the pain had been located, the problem was identified. But in order to correct the problem, surgery was required. When I emerged from the surgical anesthesia, there was a new pain. In fact, the new pain was in some ways far worse than the original pain that had taken me to the hospital. Eventually, of course, I healed and all the pain subsided, never to return.

Like surgery, arriving at resolution can involve even greater pain than the pain of the original conflict. Hence we sidestep genuine resolution in favor of temporary solution. We may make a unilateral determination or decision. We may determine simply not to pursue the matter further. We may resolve to avoid whatever question, circumstance, or person precipitated the conflict.

But we have not resolved the matter. We have only avoided the pain. Our differences continue unaddressed and thus unreconciled—and the conflict remains. In some instances, we can continue in this state for long periods, even for a lifetime.

If we are to overcome avoidance and engage the different and difficult ways that make for wholeness, we shall need help. We need to be assured that our turning leads to a constructive end and not to our demise. We need the encouragement and the example of others. We need a reformed respect for the positive role of conflict and a renewed confidence in God.

In the following pages we explore the evidences of conflict in some of the stories of God's people. Portions of the Hebrew scriptures introduce early evidence of conflict and its role in the life of God's people. Examining the life and ministry of Jesus provides insight into the conflict that surrounded him and was bequeathed to those of us who follow him. Sampling the chronicles of the early church and the letters of advice and pastoral guidance circulated among the earliest Christian congregations, we may discover the conflict that was present among them from the outset.

With this history as a foundation, a look at our present predicament invites us to consider why we find ourselves in this place, and to ask what this may suggest of God's desire for us. Finally, looking anew at conflict, not as a problem to be solved but as an opportunity to be seized, may help us to accept conflict as a gift to be pressed into service in the daily task of doing God's work as God's faithful people.

Conflict, then, entails more than resolution. Conflict invites us to *revolution*. Revolution, like its theological cousin, repentance, suggests a turning that points us and moves us in a new direction. It calls us into the continual process of change that is life itself.

We measure the movement of engines in revolutions. In an electrical motor, the alternating opposition and attraction of positive and negative magnetic poles causes a rotor to turn, producing motion that can be converted to many uses. Similarly, the combustion engines that power our cars depend on the force of a gasoline explosion pushing against a piston. Several pistons along a rod, timed to fire at regular intervals, turn a shaft which, through a system of gears, turns the wheels (revolution) and moves us along.

The succession of conflicts encountered in our lives can also be a force for movement and growth. Each time one person's uniqueness strikes hard against another person's uniqueness, conflict is encountered. As we continue to work toward resolution and even reconciliation, we find that the commonalities we share compel us toward one another even as the differences between us repel us from one another, sending us back again and again to reexamine, reaffirm, or renounce our similarities and our differences.

The Christian life is also "revolutionary," a turning charted in the cycles of life that, like the ever-turning earth, moves from day to night to day again, yet remains securely tethered to God. The Christian revolution moves from life to death to life, the movement of a people engaged, even fueled, by conflict, yet never ultimately destroyed by it.

So while we may resolve specific conflicts, we can never see the end of conflict itself. Indeed, the anticipated end of conflict, in human experience, is itself a conflict—the ultimate contention of life and death within our own bodies. Yet, for the Christian, even that conflict does not end all forceful striking together of differences. For the Christian believes that death is not the final victor. Death ultimately contends with life in God, and we are rendered changed yet again. Life is restored in resurrection, and we continue in relationship, each of us different from the other and all of us different from God. And so shall we be turned.

Chapter 1
Bred in the Bone

THE TROUBLE BEGAN WITH EDEN. It ought not surprise the modern believer that the conflicts we know at present find their origin in God. After all, we profess belief in God who made all things. So it is in God's abundant creativity that we find the raw material of conflict. Our ancestors in faith struggled, as we do, to make sense of their experience, including their experience of conflict. The stories they bequeathed us attempt to articulate in comprehensible images the mysteries we can never wholly prove.

If the Creation has any utilitarian foundation, it is probably God's desire for relationship. There is, of course, God's impulse, God's desire to be creative, a characteristic obviously shared with humankind. And there is purposefulness in just being creative, in making beauty and order. But God's own hunger for relationship stands at the base of our creation and remains the foundation of God's faithfulness to a people whose fickle infidelity is not just legendary, but documented history.

The prerequisite of relationship is the Other. To be in relationship, we must have some Other with whom and to whom to relate, one who is different from ourselves, one who is other than we. The narrative of Creation (Genesis 1 and 2) reveals the tension of otherness that holds the whole order in balance. When God began the creative process, there was neither form nor anything to be formed. There was only darkness. God's first act was to call forth that which was other than darkness: light. Having established that which was other than darkness, God then "separated the light from the darkness," establishing their relationship by defining each as separate, and therefore different, from the other. The otherness was named, one called Day and the other called Night. With the first act of creation, God established another distinction—the distinction between timelessness and time itself. Having declared the light "Day"

9

and the darkness "Night," God passed the first *evening* and the first *morning*, thus creating the first *day*.

The second day, like the first, was given to the act of separating, of making distinct, the waters above from the waters below. The waters above were given the name "Sky," while the waters below remained unnamed. On the third day, the waters below were separated into "Seas" in order to make room for the dry land called "Earth." Earth was further enriched by relationship with vegetation. The fourth day was given to the making of lights "to separate the day from the night," a sun to delineate day, a moon to delineate night. They are created, says the narrative, "to separate the light from the darkness."

In the fifth day, the realms of Sky and Sea, like Earth before them, are enriched by relationship with creatures. Birds are made for the Sky, "great sea monsters and every living creature that moves, with which the waters swarm" are made as gift to the Sea. Then a sixth day is given to enhancing Earth with creatures other than vegetation: "cattle and creeping things and wild animals of the earth of every kind." Each is presumably different from the other, each set into relationship with the other.

In the first chapter of Genesis, the creation of man and woman is of a piece with the creation of other living beings, with one distinction: man and woman are created in God's image. Man and woman are created to be creative creatures, to share the creative characteristics of God, as well as the relational characteristics. In this distinction, man and woman are made other than the plants and animals and creeping things. They are different from everything else. They are different from God.

This difference from God becomes clearer in the second narrative of Creation, which comprises the second chapter of Genesis. In that story, the longing of God is palpable. The story opens with a created world only beginning to take shape. There are Earth and Heaven, but "no plant of the field was yet in earth and no herb of the field had yet sprung up—for the Lord God had not caused it to rain upon the earth, and there was no one to till the ground." It sounds a rather empty place, and sad.

God is intimately involved with this creation, barren though it is. In this story, God does not merely call life into being, God and Creation are tangibly interactive. God touches the dust of the earth, takes it up and breathes life into it, creating Man as living being. A garden is planted around this person, and thus the teeming riches of earth's resources are set in relationship to this new creature. Vegetation "pleasant to the sight and good for food" is made to ornament the barren landscape and to sustain human life. Rivers are made to nourish the vegetation.

Man is placed in the midst of the lavish garden God has made. If this creature is to be other than God, however, it needs something more. To be wholly other, to stand against God in relationship, this creature must have freedom. That freedom is only tentatively granted as God offers Man freedom to eat of every kind of tree, save one. That freedom is also limited by the bounds of the garden itself.

Still, God is not satisfied. Something is missing. Man, too, needs tangible company. Wild beasts and birds are made and brought to Man to be named, but no real companion seems to emerge from the lot. So God reaches into Man himself and takes a portion of Man and makes it distinct from Man. From that portion, God fashions a creature which, while like Man, is Other. When this creature is brought to Man, Man names the creature Woman. Man is now in relationship with God and with Woman.

But Man's sense of otherness is only partly formed. Indeed, when Man names Woman, he declares, "This at last is bone of my bones and flesh of my flesh." Thus Man sees in Woman only their similarities, their sameness. This point is perhaps amplified by a nakedness in which they felt no shame. While Man and Woman are distinctly different from one another, they are not yet conscious of their otherness. Indeed, there seems no conscious awareness of difference among the three principals: God, Man, and Woman.

With the eating of the forbidden fruit, conscious difference emerges (Genesis 3). Man and Woman are now not just aware of otherness, but of difference. They see that difference in their nakedness, and they seek to hide themselves. And they also hide from God. They are suddenly aware, in a way they had not experienced previously, that God is different. The difference repels one from the other. Man and Woman are separated from each other in clothing, and separated from God by the underbrush. God is separated from Man and Woman by expelling them from the garden.

Man and Woman are not the only ones to experience the consequences of freedom in this story. God, too, learns the cost of relationship with the Other. God experiences hurt and manifests that hurt in anger, introducing a new word into the vocabulary of relationship: enmity. "I will put enmity between you and the woman," says God to the serpent, "and between your offspring and hers; he shall strike at your head, and you shall strike at his heel" (Genesis 3:15). Up to this point, all elements of creation were bound in common friendship. Plants, animals, humans—all of nature—and God were bound in a relationship defined by cooperative mutuality. But in the breaching of that cooperation, enmity enters. To Adam God says, ". . . cursed is the ground because of you; in toil you shall eat of it all the days of your life" (Genesis 3:17). The relationship between humankind and nature will no longer be marked by cooperation, but by struggle.

Enmity means "not friend." In introducing enmity, God pronounces that those who had been created to be friend to one another and to God are deemed "not friend." In this story, God echoes a plaintive but familiar cry; "You are not my friend" is a common response of the child. Our earliest assumptions of trust are predicated upon conformity to one will. So long as the other person goes along with me, conforms to my will, we are friends. But the moment the other exerts an independent will—the moment the other exercises the distinction of otherness—we are no longer friends. Yet it is precisely this free expression of otherness, this difference, that makes true friendship, and genuine love, possible.

In their disobedience, Man and Woman finally become fully Other than God. Man is not given a proper name until the fateful eating of the forbidden fruit. Only after God has pronounced their enmity is the Man referred to as Adam and the woman, Eve. Despite the stinging pain of their disobedience, God nevertheless fashions clothes for Adam and Eve, either because God feels tenderly toward them even in displeasure and disappointment, or because God cannot bear the sight of their nakedness which now so boldly declares their difference—for these reasons and more, or for reasons beyond our knowing.

Then, in a final act of separation, God sets Adam and Eve apart from the garden. Their freedom is no longer bounded by its limits. They are now free to walk away from God. Difficult as it must be for them all, this moment is essential to whatever will follow. For unless they are free to walk away, they are not free to choose to stay. Their independent exercise of will in an act of disobedience teaches them and God the painful consequences of otherness and the difficult demands of love.

It would seem, however, that while God is rudely educated and painfully smitten by this experience with Man and Woman, Adam and Eve are as yet largely ignorant of the consequences of their independence. Following the birth of Cain and Abel, Adam and Eve experience the painful and disappointing consequences of freedom when one of the children of their procreation exerts a destructive and willful independence, killing the other (Genesis 4).

The sons of Adam and Eve are very different. Abel grows up to be a shepherd, Cain a farmer. When each makes offering to God, God distinguishes between them, accepting the offering of Abel, but ignoring the offering of Cain. In Cain's response, jealousy enters the catalog of human emotions. God sees the distress of Cain and counsels him to be less resentful of Abel, more accepting of his own differentness, and more confident of his own worth, but to no avail. In his jealousy and anger, Cain attacks Abel and kills him. Thus do Adam and Eve experience the pain of human will and human freedom in the loss of a son.

The volatile mixture of freedom and otherness seem to generate conflict. As the world grew more populous and the creativity unleashed in God's initiative brought forth diversity, conflict between human beings increased. It became so painful that God could not endure it. As the Genesis account has it, God actually regretted having made humankind (6:7).

Who has not known in the complexity of human relationships the sad disappointment of love, the emotional fallout of conflict? With it comes regret at risking any relationship and the sincere desire to be rid of relationships' bother. God determined to be done with the project of relationship (Genesis 6:6-7). God would purge the earth of humankind, beasts, birds, and creeping things. But even in the depths of sadness, God's hope was touched by the simple faith of Noah. So even before God could execute the extreme desire to be done with it all, a new plan was considered. A few would be saved and God would try again.

Under the new plan, Noah and his family would be spared, as would representative pairs of all the created animals. Difference would be preserved not only among the surviving humans, but among all the species of animals. The essential otherness born of created differences would survive the flood.

But otherness was mitigated by the gift of common language. Though different in themselves, people could, by means of language, transcend their differences and find unity. Noah's descendants increased and eventually settled in a valley in the land of Shinar. They learned to make bricks and mortar and to exercise their own creativity. They determined to build a city and, in that city, "a tower with its top in the heavens" (Genesis 11). The purpose of their grand scheme was to "make a name" for themselves. It seems innocent enough, this little burst of civic pride. But the motive drew God's ire.

When I was a child and heard the story of the Tower of Babel, I was told that the object of this structure was to reach high into the sky, even to the throne of God. If that was the motive for its building, then it is clear that those involved desired to make their own power, achievement, and authority the equal to God's. But it seems that what the builders had in mind was an achievement to distinguish themselves. They did not want the tower because it was useful or necessary to their common life; they wanted it because it was a tangible sign of their difference from everyone else around them. No other nation would have such a tower, but would envy them their tower and covet it. Perhaps other nations would see this tower and fear those who had built it.

For either reason, or both, God was not pleased. If this is how they used the gifts that make for unity—only to build for greater disunity—then the gift would be remanded. Their common language was taken away, and in its place they were given yet another challenge to unity in the confusion of different languages.

These stories of the work of communities of believers like us—people struggling to come to terms with the forces of conflict and their own human nature—assure us that our present dilemmas are not wholly unique to human experience. This is reassuring good news, especially when we are feeling overwhelmed and despair that we might be subsumed by our present conflicts. In these stories we see others at the task of discerning the roots of our human conflict and finding a foundation for our difficulties in the fabric of creation itself.

Moreover, these stories are but chapters in the one story encompassed by the biblical scriptures. This larger, longer story invites us to walk the path of a people that parallels the path of each person, a path of action and awareness from creation and origin through death and beyond. These are a story and a path across a varied topography, a landscape of life's hills and valleys. But we see, as we make the journey, that conflict—or at least, the potential for conflict—is built into the very structures of life. That being the case, how are we to live? We return to the story for insight into that question.

Relatedness was not enough. Something more was needed. So God offered a formal commitment to particular relationship with the people. God invited Abram and Sarai to leave what was familiar and venture into an unknown—which is to say, they were invited to enter into a relationship (Genesis 12-18). Every relationship is a venture that beckons us from the familiar into the unknown. The relationship between Abram, Sarai, and God would be based on a covenant, a promise. In token of their new relationship, Abram would henceforth be named Abraham and Sarai would be named Sarah. God promised to be with Abraham and Sarah and with their descendants forever.

With their relationship so clearly established, they would always have the promise to come back to in times of difficulty. When conflict threatened to separate them, they would be reminded that their differences were based in the very otherness that made their relationship possible. But they were also reminded that whatever difference separated them was transcended by the promise that established their relationship.

As Abraham's heirs increased, the differences between them

became points of contention. Like Cain and Abel before them, the brothers Jacob and Esau succumbed to jealousy (Genesis 25:19ff). Yet there is a striking difference between the stories of these two pairs of contentious brothers, one that suggests a growing insight into how such differences might be mediated. The outcome of the conflict between Jacob and Esau was not fatal, but it was marked by a long-standing estrangement between the two. After many years of separation, Jacob proposed to meet Esau (Genesis 27—33).

As he reached the ford in the river that separated him from his brother, Jacob was worried. He had just received word that Esau was approaching and that he had four hundred men with him. All the old times came back to haunt Jacob. Every buried memory rushed forth, as real and present as the day of their happening. The very land to which he was returning was his only because of a bowl of food and an old sheepskin. The way he had tricked Esau out of his birthright was as vivid as ever in his own mind. He remembered how hungry Esau had been the day he had come in from the hunt, and how good his own stew must have smelled to the hungry man. Taking advantage of Esau's weakness—his slow wit made slower now by hunger and fatigue—Jacob bartered a bowl of stew for his older brother's birthright.

Later, Jacob sealed this informal bargain. He ensured that Esau's privileges as the elder brother would come into his own possession. If he could secure his father's blessing—the blessing by which his father, Isaac, would transmit the inheritance to Esau—Jacob would be guaranteed what Esau had so casually promised over that bowl of stew. With the help of his cunning mother, Jacob literally pulled the wool over his own eyes, drawing a sheepskin over his smooth neck and back. Jacob knelt before Isaac in Esau's place, passing himself off as his hirsute brother, and Isaac pronounced the words of blessing. The words could not be recalled. Jacob had dishonestly secured his father's blessing, the blessing and the land that belonged to the elder Esau.

Jacob was a self-made man who knew how to work the system. He had it all. But as he approached home and confrontation with Esau, his self-confidence began to disintegrate.

Under cover of darkness, Jacob crossed the river. Once the wives, the children, the livestock, and the goods had safely forded, he sent them on ahead. But he paused at the water's edge in the darkness.

He was alone and the preoccupations of the crossing were behind him. The water, too, was behind him—no longer a protective moat, but a dangerous barrier that placed him squarely at Esau's mercy. The night by the river was probably the single most important night in Jacob's life. In that night he matured, and his name was changed, signifying that when the morning broke he would no longer be the same person. Whatever it was that wrought the change was in that night.

In a wrestling match that lasted throughout the night, Jacob's antagonist was a mysterious other man, a being in human form. Some say the mysterious wrestler was God. Jacob seems to have thought so, for he named the place Peniel, meaning "the face of God." It does seem fair to say that what Jacob encountered was reality. He was made to face that which he would rather have ignored, that which he probably *had* ignored right up to the moment it took hold of him and refused to let him go.

The conflict between Jacob and the stranger was neither an attack nor an ambush. But whatever it was, it was certainly decisive, a deliberate test of strength. Something grabbed hold of Jacob and, with a wrench, it pulled. As the struggle progressed, a dialogue began. The stranger was having difficulty throwing Jacob. The opponent touched Jacob's thigh, and pain coursed through Jacob's body. But still neither would loosen his grip. As the pain pierced Jacob, he heard the stranger ask, "What is your name?" Without thought or hesitation, Jacob told him.

As the syllables passed from his lips, Jacob was defeated. The name of a person was as sacred as the soul. To possess a person's name was to take hold of that person's most precious possession, and the stranger had just taken Jacob's name. As the gray haze of morning crept in around them, Jacob tried to regain his loss. With plaintive determination, Jacob held fast to his partner and begged, "Please tell me your name."

When the stranger spoke again, it was not to give any advantage to Jacob. Instead, the stranger took away Jacob's name forever. Jacob was given a new name, the name Israel, to signify that he had struggled with God and with the reality of his own life, and that he would never be the same again.

Jacob staggered away from the conflict whole but hurt. He had wrestled with reality, he had been tumbled by truth. The closer he drew now to Esau and to the truth of his past, the humbler his steps became. The determined swagger of the self-made man was gone. He would never walk upright again. Every step would be uneasy, and every time that particular foot touched the ground, the weight of his body would send the pain shooting through his side to remind him. He to whom everything had come so easily would now have to consider every step lest he stumble and fall. But the pain was the gift, the only tangible thing he took from that night. As Noah had been given a rainbow in token of God's mercy, so Jacob was given the pain to remember always the need of that mercy. Jacob came away from the river a new person.

When Jacob and Esau finally met, it was a meeting of reconciling love. Jacob was not the person Esau had known. Esau could see even from a distance that Jacob was changed. Running out to meet him, Esau embraced his brother and kissed him. They wept together. Then Esau said, "Let us set out, and I will go at your pace." Out of his conflict, Jacob found a new identity, and he found his brother.

In time, Israel—the descendants of Jacob—became a nation, a distinct people with their own identity. Defining the boundaries that distinguish who we are and how we shall behave helps us live in the midst of others, helps us live with the differences that separate us and the conflicts that challenge us.

In Egypt, life was defined for the people of Israel; they lived as slaves (Exodus 1). When they were delivered from slavery in Egypt, God's people left behind the cruel institution of imposed slavery (Exodus 14—15:21). But they also left behind the relative security of that estate. In the uncharted unknown of the desert, they complained and begged to return (Exodus 16—17:7).

The Decalogue—the Ten Commandments—help to define

who God's people are and how their lives are lived (Exodus 20). The commandments begin with the specific identification of Israel's God as the God who brought them out of Egypt. Israel is distinct among other peoples because Israel has only one God, a God without likeness (whose distinction cannot be captured, rendered, or duplicated). Israel is distinct among other peoples because Israel will not worship other gods. Moreover, when God's people swear or take an oath invoking the name of God, that oath is considered inviolate.

Israel is distinct in the rhythm of its life. The people labor six days in succession, but reserve the seventh day as a sabbath, a day of rest, quiet, and meditation. In this manner they pattern their life on God's model, ordering their time as God ordered time in the days of Creation.

In these distinctions, the relationship between God and the people is defined and given structure. The commandments then turn to the matter of other relationships: relationships to neighbor and self.

The relationship between parents and offspring is to be one of respect. Age and experience are to be honored, and parents, especially, are to be valued by their children. Even in our contemporary experience, those who practice such respect are notable. In any time or culture where human value depends on physical productivity and where youthful vitality is deemed superior, a high regard for the aged is distinctive.

The practice of murder is prohibited, not because it is an expression of violence but because it is the ultimate expression of disrespect for human life individually and in community. To take or deny another human life is to pronounce as worthless and unnecessary that which God has created. The prohibition against murder extends beyond the physical taking of life to the many expressions of disrespect by which we render a person worthless. To demean the contribution of another, or to deny that contribution by ignoring, silencing, or preventing it, is to practice a kind of bloodless murder, damaging to the individual and to the community. To eliminate or frustrate another human life is obviously harmful to the individual victim. But it is also a source of pain and loss to the larger community, those who are bound in love and kinship to the victim and benefit from relationship with the victim. Since the people of God assert that all human life proceeds from the creative hand of God, then all human life is knit together in a common kinship. Therefore, any diminishment of life is a diminishment of the whole human family.

The prohibition of adultery is only partially concerned with sexual morality. Israel's life is defined by promise, by covenant. A substance is adulterated when its purity is altered by the addition of some different substance. To make a promise, then to compromise the original intent of that promise, is an adulteration of the promise. The marital vows, for example, include the promise to confine all genital expressions of intimacy to the singular relationship with the marriage partner. Thus, compromising the marital vow by indulging a genital expression of intimacy with someone outside that exclusive relationship is a compromise of the original promise. The act is a corruption of a pure relationship and a corruption of the human bodies involved, but the most grievous adulteration is the adulteration of the promise. The original promise of fidelity is debased by the violation.

Adultery, therefore, extends to many more situations than the genital, even within the context of marriage. Any violation of the promise to love and respect one's marriage partner is an adultery as illicit as any sexual compromise. The distinction between these adulteries is not in degree, but only in kind. The prohibition of adultery is applicable to all facets of the covenant promise. One biblical definition of adultery is "idolatry." Idolatry is an obvious corruption of the covenant promises to have no other gods and to neither fashion nor worship images of the one God.

While marriage is certainly one of the more prominent expressions of covenant relationship between human beings, it is still secondary and less widely experienced among Christians than the covenant of baptism. Since marriage is experienced only by those called to that estate, extending the prohibition of adultery to the covenant promises of baptism certainly makes adultery a matter of immediacy to all Christians. In the prohibition of adultery the community honors its promises. Adulterating one's promise erodes integrity. Renegotiating a promise has far greater integrity than compromising the promise; a divorce is more honorable than taking a secret partner on the side.

This principle has profound consequences in times of conflict between people who have shared a long and close relationship with one another, which is often the case within the church. It is essential to be clear about our promises and to be clear in our expectations of one another. When we encounter differences between us, as inevitably we shall, we may honestly confront those differences and either recommit to our relationship or renegotiate it. But we are not free to adulterate that relationship by circumnavigating the covenant we have with each other, and with God.

The people of God do not steal. Whatever they possess, either individually or as a nation, is honestly gained and secured. A standard of fairness and justice, honest wages for honest work, a fair price for quality goods, define their commerce with one another and with others. The prohibition of theft reveals a profound ecology. Everything proceeds from God's bountiful creativity. God's free choice to give so generous a gift is assurance of sufficient means to live and eliminates any need to steal for survival. Moreover, the tendency to confuse need and greed requires constant reassurance that God will provide, obviating the need to take from one another, or from creation itself, more than one's allotted share.

Prohibiting false witness against the neighbor distinguishes the people of God as honest and fair in their assessments of others. They seek the truth about those who are different from them, rather than rely on false perceptions, assumptions, or reports. They are thoughtful and measured in their judgments of others, resisting the easy temptation to indulge stereotypes and prejudices.

Finally, the people of God measure their own worth on the basis of God's love and respect for them, not upon material possession. Their lives are not driven by envy of others, but by love and gratitude for God. As important as this principle was to a people recently released from slavery and presumably poor, it became all the more important whenever one or all of them achieved worldly success.

Even in receiving and implementing these principles, conflict arose. As Moses prepared to bring these principles before the people, the people themselves were gathering their jewelry and fashioning a golden calf (Exodus 32). While we cannot be sure exactly what the actions of the people and their calf were intended to mean, we can be quite certain that their confrontation with Moses was a rousing conflict, a forceful striking together of two very different perspectives. The force was formidable. When the dust settled, the tablets of stone containing the ten principles lay in rubble. The people, their golden calf literally ground into dust, were forced to eat their idol.

Ultimately, the Decalogue prevailed. The people fashioned a life together, in God. Their story unfolds in Exodus, Leviticus, Numbers, and Deuteronomy. In that story we meet a people living slowly but steadfastly into relationship with God. As in any relationship, there are moments of conflict. But they return again and again to the basic principles of the Decalogue, shaping their life and their relationships according to those fundamental understandings.

In the book of Deuteronomy (chapters 5 and following), the Decalogue reappears. In the time that Deuteronomy was recorded, the nation of Israel had ended its exodus journey and had settled. Indeed, the people of Israel were experiencing considerable prosperity. Yet the people are exhorted anew. They are reminded of their history and the Decalogue is repeated. Furthermore, they are given a central text and tenet of their tradition when they are commanded, "Hear, O Israel: The Lord is our God, the Lord alone. You shall love the Lord your God with all your heart, and with all your soul, and with all your might" (Deut. 6:4-5). This bold reiteration suggests that the people, in the midst of their prosperity and comfort, had lost sight of the source of their bounty. They had strayed from the covenant. They needed reminding.

The book of Deuteronomy ends the five-volume history of Israel's beginnings and concludes with the death of Moses and the transmission of responsibility to Joshua. There follows a succession of narratives detailing the struggle of relationship, the continuing relationship of God and Israel. The experience of

Joshua and the line of prophets and kings who succeed him is little different from the experience of Moses: the conflict enjoined when God and humankind encounter their differences.

External conflicts of war and similar acts of violence continue in the writings of the prophets. There are other conflicts, too, conflicts not as blatantly violent, but no less important in their consequences. Conflict and covenant also have intimate and personal dimensions.

The story of Hosea is one of tremendous personal suffering. Hosea is less familiar to us than Job, whose persecutions and tribulations are legendary. Hosea marries a woman named Gomer, who bears three children. Each birth is more bittersweet than the last, for Gomer is given to prostitution. The conflict between Hosea and Gomer and the struggle they engender become, for Hosea, a way of understanding the conflicted tension between God and Israel. Infidelity fills the pages of their story.

Gomer, whose proclivity toward prostitution seems uncontrollable, repeatedly violates the covenant of marital fidelity. Again and again, she retreats to habitual, casual sex. Again and again, Hosea seeks her out and brings her home. We cannot know whether Hosea and Gomer are historical characters, but we do know that for the author of the story Hosea embodies the steadfastness of God. Gomer personifies the infidelities of Israel, whose devotion to God is compromised by attraction to the gods of other, rival religions.

The story of Hosea and Gomer casts the relationship and the conflict between God and Israel in the language of conjugal intimacy. The images so common to other conceptualizations of the God/human relationship suggest that it is like the blood kinship of parent and child. The book of Hosea, rather, suggests that the relationship between God and humankind is not that of parent and child, but the relationship of promise, the covenant that characterizes the marital union.

Conflict between parent and child is, naturally, different from conflict between spouses. Fundamentally, there is the difference of blood kinship versus covenant kinship. As the aphorism maintains, blood is thicker than water (and probably always has been). Certain duties, rights, and privileges pertain to the blood relationship that are not associated with other kinds of relationship.

The marital relationship, on the other hand, is based not upon blood but on promise. Indeed, consanguinity—blood relationship—forbids marriage between certain relatives, as a preventative against the biological hazards of congenital defect and against the social hazards of incest. Marriages are made *across* bloodlines, thus establishing distinct *difference* between the two partners in the union. It is only out of such distinct biological difference that healthy new life is conceived and born.

But the willing embrace of such difference comes neither naturally nor easily to us. To navigate the complications of such human difference, we negotiate and order these relationships by the covenant agreement called marriage. In that covenant, we establish the principles of difference and we articulate the expectations of union. We acknowledge that there are profound differences between the partners. We acknowledge that these differences demand the best efforts of each partner and require the support of a much larger community. And we articulate the principles of love, fidelity, mutual respect, forgiveness, and interdependence that guide us through the difficult process of lifelong covenant in intimate relationship.

The story of Hosea and Gomer provides a model of relationship that respects the difficulties and demands of covenant. The painful differences between Hosea and Gomer, like the painful differences between God and God's people, are not resolved. All does not end neatly or happily. Neither Gomer nor Israel repents and conforms to the standards of fidelity demanded of covenant. But neither Hosea nor God relents and compromises those standards. The conflicts are not resolved.

While we do not see resolution, we do see resolve in the steadfast commitment of both Hosea and God. Each remains committed to the covenant. Each seeks out the wayward partner. Each reaffirms the promise to be faithful to that partner, despite the partner's wanderings. Yet each also yearns for an equal commitment, a requital. Still, the loving commitment of neither Hosea nor God is requited. The story, like life itself, remains open ended.

Conflict, then, is part of the dynamic of living. While it may not be the desired outcome of relationship, conflict is the ever-present product of our difference, our otherness. The story of Hosea and Gomer acknowledges this reality without attempting to impose a false order on it.

The four brief chapters of the tale of Jonah barely fill three pages in most modern bibles. Yet this short story bristles with conflict. The action and the characters are colorful and vivid. Jonah, the captain and his shipmates, the big fish, the city of Nineveh, the protecting plant, and God are all impressive. Despite, or perhaps because of, the physicality of the story, it remains a splendid and lively account of a different kind of conflict—the conflict of vocation. Yet this is not a story of the interior struggles of personal conflict. Instead of revealing to us such internal conflict, the story of Jonah shows the external consequences of vocational conflict.

The story begins with Jonah and God. God has called Jonah and asked him to go to Nineveh, where he is to pronounce God's judgment upon that city. The mission is very clear, far clearer than any of us experience in the course of vocational discernment. Jonah is told exactly where he is to go and exactly what he is to do.

But there is a conflict of wills. God desires that Jonah do one thing; Jonah desires to do something quite different. Instead of going to Nineveh as requested, Jonah heads in the opposite direction, traveling to Joppa, a port city, where he finds a ship going out to sea.

Once aboard, Jonah goes to sleep—hardly the condition of a man deeply conflicted over his mission. But the sea is ripped by tempest and the ship is soon in danger of breaking up. Jonah remains asleep, untouched by the upheaval he has created in the world around him. Lives and property are in grave danger. Jonah is awakened by the captain and crew, who have exhausted themselves trying to stay afloat. It occurs to them that the stranger in their hold may have something to do with their plight. They confront Jonah and he confesses that he is, indeed, the problem. The solution, Jonah suggests, is to throw him overboard.

The ship's captain and crew, themselves followers of other gods, are nonetheless concerned that they not take Jonah's life, the almost certain outcome of surrendering him to the violent seas. Before they throw Jonah overboard, they beg God not to account them guilty of murder. They acknowledge that it is clearly by God's will that this predicament is upon them and Jonah. Then they surrender Jonah to the waves, which is to say, they do for Jonah what he will not do of his own accord; they surrender him to God's will.

Jonah does not drown, but is swallowed up by a big fish. After three days and three nights, Jonah relents. He will do as God has requested. God commands the fish to spew Jonah out upon dry land. Jonah is expelled, and God repeats the commission that he go to Nineveh and pronounce judgment.

Jonah goes to Nineveh and pronounces God's judgment. The people of Nineveh believe Jonah, and they repent immediately. God accepts their repentance, but Jonah is outraged. Neither Nineveh nor God has acted according to Jonah's will. The story has not turned out as he expected. He expected the people to be resistant, even as he had been resistant, for this certainly would have vindicated his earlier judgment of his mission. He also expected that for their resistance, the people of Nineveh would suffer disaster as he had. Jonah expected his will to be confirmed, but it was not.

Depressed by the outcome, Jonah retreats outside the city and makes camp. He waits with grim determination to see his will come to fruition, but it does not. As a lesson, God causes a plant to grow up over Jonah's hut, a plant that provides welcome shade from the sun's heat. Jonah appreciates the plant not only for the comfort, but for the company, for there is no other living thing in his life. When Jonah feels affection and gratitude for the plant, God causes the plant to die. When Jonah protests, God uses the plant as a parable to illustrate that just as Jonah cared for the plant, so God cared for the people of Nineveh.

Like the story of Hosea, the story of Jonah is not neatly resolved. The conflict of wills remains. Jonah is so disappointed, he begs to die. His will is so strong that he would rather die than capitulate. It matters nothing to him that his willfulness has endangered the lives of innocent people, both on ship-board and in Nineveh itself. It matters little to him that his willfulness has upset the natural order, stirring up the winds and sea and inflicting indigestion upon a fish. It matters only to him that his will has not prevailed. The story ends in impasse, Jonah stubbornly unrepentant, his will and God's will conflicting.

The foregoing are but a few evidences of the many in Hebrew scriptures that conflict has been part of the life of God's people from the earliest intimations of their relationship with God. Within the imaginative explorations into human origins and experiences, the rich stories of human and historical relation-ships, and the poetic utterances to a God who is gradually revealed, as each of us is to the other—in the daily unfolding of life—we see that difference and conflict are essential, inevitable components of being. They are as necessary to our life as water, fire, and air. And like these powerful elements, whose various combinations and admixtures can mean either life or death for us, difference and conflict demand our respect. They have the power to sustain life, and to destroy it.

Chapter 2
The Trouble With Jesus

MATTHEW, MARK, LUKE, AND JOHN—these four different gospels, by four different authors were written from four different cultural, geographical, and theological perspectives at four different times. Everything we know of Jesus is founded upon and frustrated by these differences. All the information we have about Jesus is riddled with conflict. There are differences in detail, presentation, and interpretation, sometimes even of the same event.

Those who assembled the scriptures valued the differences represented in the texts as acceptable, perhaps even desirable. After all, do not the same inconsistencies mark our own experience? Any four letters of reference for the same person will likely vary. Ask any four people to describe someone or something, and you will probably get four different descriptions. The resulting discrepancies may all be legitimate if we accept that they represent genuine differences of opinion and perspective.

Part of the trouble with Jesus, then, is that what we know of him is derived from different testimonies drawn from different sources at different times, and sometimes at considerable distance from Jesus himself. We can be (and sometimes are) frustrated by this reality. But the differences themselves indicate a respect for the variances they represent, a respect for varied testimony and witness as essential to our knowledge. The differences make the person of Jesus accessible. In that he was born to an aged father and a youthful mother, into a culture that was both Jewish and Roman, and practiced a ministry that embraced the experience of rich and poor, nearly everyone of his own day and ours can find a point of connection to the person and the story of Jesus. Moreover, the differences reflected in each gospel writer's account suggest that Jesus was as complex as any of us—that ambiguity, paradox, and mystery accompanied his life and actions even as they accompany ours.

At least two of the gospels—Matthew and John—are accounts of Jesus' life and ministry that are intentionally provocative. Each of these gospels was written to refute specific differences of opinion. Each is a document defending a particular point of view at conflict with an opposing perspective.

The gospel according to Matthew is set in the midst of controversy. A central concern of this gospel account is the reform of Judaism. At many points in Matthew's gospel the teaching of Jesus is deliberately set against the prevailing practice of the time.

"Do not think that I have come to abolish the law or the prophets" says Jesus. "I have come not to abolish but to fulfill" (Matthew 5:17). This remark, made at the commencement of his public ministry, is followed thereafter by the frequent formula, "You have heard that it was said, . . . But I say to you." In this manner, Jesus is characterized as one who confronts, challenges, and re-forms the accepted norm.

In the first centuries after their experience of Jesus, as the surviving communities of believers struggled to comprehend the meaning of that experience, there were differences of opinion and outright conflicts. The most contentious dispute centered on the meaning of Jesus within Judaism and the meaning of Jesus to all those outside Judaism. That tension is reflected in the gospel according to Matthew.

The calling of Matthew himself touches another sore spot—the conflict between Jews and their Roman rulers (Matthew 9:9-13). Matthew was called to discipleship from his place "at the tax booth," where he made his living as an employee of the Roman government. As a Jew in the employ of the occupying imperial government, Matthew personifies a deeply entrenched religious and political conflict. When Jesus invites Matthew into his circle, and immediately accompanies Matthew to dinner with Matthew's tax collector friends and colleagues, the controversy is engaged. Jesus draws the criticism of the Pharisees as surely as the rod attracts lightning.

However, this engagement of and identification with outcasts is important to our understanding of what Jesus meant to the community represented in the gospel of Matthew. At one level, perhaps, they were concerned to portray Jesus as sympathetic to their point of view, to claim Jesus as "on their side."

The desire to co-opt Jesus as advocate is certainly a part of the legacy we inherit.

But such claims need not always lead to exclusivity. Matthew was one of twelve very different disciples. At the very least, the call of Matthew and the other eleven reminds us that Jesus obviously tolerated, even embraced, a range of difference beyond the customary.

The gospel according to John, like the gospel of Matthew, is the product of particular conflict. Of the four gospels, John's is the last one written. It is, then, furthest removed in time from the actual experience of Jesus. Evidence suggests that it was written not as the account of a single author, but as the collective witness of a community of Christians whose life was shaped by the influence or memory of a disciple named John, also known as "the beloved disciple" of Jesus.

The inference that Jesus expressed a preference for one disciple over another, and for John in particular, is clearly evident in the "beloved" disciple from whose perspective the gospel of John is cast. This claim to preferred status tells us less about Jesus' affections than about the need of the authors to establish their own authority. Just as the community of Matthew's gospel was concerned to portray Jesus as "on their side," so the community of John's gospel claims authority by placing John at the privileged side of Jesus.

By the time the gospel according to John was written, a number of communities of followers had formed around the memory of Jesus. Few, if any, of those so gathered had actually met Jesus. Each, however, was concerned to articulate what Jesus meant to them individually and what Jesus meant to them as a community. Each was influenced by the memory and testimony of a particular person or perspective. Some gathered around the person or memory of Peter, others around John, Matthew, and numerous other charismatic figures who rose to prominence in the first or second generation of witnesses to the person and the "phenomenon" of Jesus.

It is important to understand that Jesus is both person and phenomenon. What we know of Jesus and what we know of any human being is not limited to what we know of the person. There is also what we deduce from the interactions of that person with other persons, places, things, and events. The greater part of what we know of anyone consists of what is revealed in those interactions.

Thus, those who sought to understand the meaning of Jesus derived that meaning not only from what they knew of his person and what was related by witnesses who shared close relationships with him, but also from what was deduced about Jesus from his interactions with everyone and everything around him. This knowledge is sometimes revealed in the corroborated accounts of specific events in the life of Jesus recounted in the gospels. In some instances, these stories show remarkable consistency from one gospel to another. The gospel according to Mark, which is probably the oldest account, is the most straightforward. It is widely believed that the accounts of Mark, Matthew, and Luke were derived in part from an earlier account now largely lost. But whatever we know of Jesus depends on these early records.

In certain instances these accounts purport to tell us not only what we *can* know, but what we *ought* to know of Jesus. This was certainly the aim of those who composed John's gospel. By the time of its writing, opinion on what the person and phenomenon of Jesus meant was sharply divided.

Among the most powerful controversies that arose in the years following Jesus' time was the conflict between those who embraced Gnosticism and those who did not. *Gnosis* is the Greek word for "knowledge." Gnosticism is not a specific creed so much as a way of believing. Therefore, Gnostics could be pagan or Christian. The foundation of Gnosticism is the role and authority one accords to empirical knowledge. Some early Christians believed that knowledge of God had been imparted to certain of the apostles, and thus to their followers, by secret or privileged means. For them the apostle whose teachings they acknowledged must be situated within Jesus' inner circle, or given privileged access to information imparted by Jesus.

Gnosticism can influence one's philosophy, theology, anthropology, psychology, and morality. But here we consider those who interpreted Jesus through the system of Gnosticism and those who did not. In the first two centuries after Jesus the division between these groups became a central concern. The authors of John's gospel refute the arguments of the Gnostic Christians. Much of the gospel according to John, then, is itself a well-constructed argument. Of all the gospel accounts, it is the most "interpretive."

The gospel of John provides little unadorned reporting. More frequently, it recounts the life and ministry of Jesus with illustrative or interpretive commentary. For example, it is reported that Jesus said, "Let anyone who is thirsty come to me, and let the one who believes in me drink. As the scripture has said, 'Out of the believer's heart shall flow rivers of living water'" (John 7:37-38). The account continues, however, with this aside: "Now he said this about the Spirit, which believers in him were to receive; for as yet there was no Spirit, because Jesus was not yet glorified" (John 7:39). The author quotes a saying attributed to Jesus and links that saying to an earlier Hebrew text. Then the author adds an interpretation that reveals a developed theology of the Holy Spirit. While this kind of interpretive addition can be found in other gospels, it is most characteristic of John's. And, of course, interpretation slants the way we read and understand stories.

The interpretive biases of the gospel accounts do not diminish their power, their authority, or their veracity. But they do present a problem, especially if one assumes that the four gospel accounts present a seamless and unbiased biography of Jesus. If, however, one accepts each account as the perceived truth of a different witness or community of witnesses, this problem is more easily counted as a gift. What emerges from the combined witness of the four gospels is a rich introduction to Jesus. We are provided with a variety of perspectives, not only of Jesus, but of our ancestral community of faith. These varied perspectives grant us insight into Jesus, but perhaps of equal importance, into each person or community whose witness is recorded. The worth of this treasure is not always appreciated, especially when we fall into disagreement over how we are to read these gospel texts.

The biblical scriptures are family history, much like that I learned of my own family. I grew up in the American South. When a member of the family or community died, people gathered in the home of the deceased. The deceased was remembered in stories that reflected many different perspectives. Sisters and brothers, often aged themselves, recounted childhood memories that allowed us to see the deceased as a child, as the son or daughter of parents. These stories were windows into the interactions of families and times long disappeared. Children of the deceased provided glimpses into the intimate moments of family. Coworkers and neighbors revealed a lifetime of habits and hurts, kindnesses and curses. Grandchildren and great-grandchildren brought their own perspectives, limited by time but sometimes rich in insight, the bonds between youth and age providing their own unique experiences. Memories occasionally clashed, but more frequently they encouraged further sharing. The tapestry of stories revealed far more of the person than any one person could have known. While each person's association with the departed differed, each had value and was accorded respect.

The practice of faith—any faith—is not just a matter of trust in a particular person or truth. The development and practice of faith is a life-long process of seeking and making meaning out of our experience. Those who wrote the gospels, and the people for whom they were recorded, were not only trying to describe who Jesus was and what Jesus did; they were very much concerned with explaining what Jesus meant to them, what difference he made in their lives, and how relationship with him and/or his story shaped life's meaning.

The scriptural stories and the many different meanings derived from those stories affirm truth's richness. When someone in attendance at my great-grandmother's wake recalled her beauty, that person certainly was not referring to the ancient woman of stout proportions, stern face, and unpredictable mood I remembered. Whose experience was true? They both were. My great-grandmother was everything I knew her to be, but she was also everything recalled by her lifelong friend. When the two truths met, they expressed a larger truth and presented a three-dimensional portrait of this woman.

More important to our purposes here, however, was that neither I nor my great-grandmother's friend fell into disagreement over our conflicting assessments of the woman we were remembering. My great-grandmother's friend saw no need to correct my memory, and I saw no purpose in contradicting hers. As we explored our experiences of my great-grandmother more fully, each of us learned something new about this woman each of us had known, but only in part.

Even when these differences are overcome, though, Jesus remains a problem. For in the memories of him that constitute the gospels, we encounter a man whose person, whose words and actions come up hard against the people and practices of his own day, and against us too.

Jesus commissioned twelve disciples to share his work. In both Matthew's gospel (10:34-39) and Luke's (Luke 12:51-53; 14:26-27), Jesus explicitly warns the disciples that association with him and his ministry will expose them to conflict. Specifically, they will encounter conflict in the closest, most intimate relationships we can know: family. Presumably, some of them had families and jobs—spouses, dependents, and colleagues—who shared neither their enthusiasm for nor their commitment to Jesus.

"Do not think that I have come to bring peace to the earth," Jesus said, "I have not come to bring peace, but a sword. For I have come to set a man against his father, and a daughter against her mother, and a daughter-in-law against her mother-in-law; and one's foes will be members of one's own household" (Matthew 10:34).

For those who endured the periodic persecutions mounted against the early Christian community, the words "I came to bring fire to the earth . . ." (Luke 12:49) gave meaning and purpose to death and destruction. The image of fire has specific meaning for the potter and the metalworker. Clay, which disintegrates in water, when glazed and fired in the kiln becomes an impervious vessel for transporting and storing the very water that would otherwise destroy it. Fire refines the conglomerated amalgam of elements long blended over time, separating those elements. Fire separates iron from the other minerals that bind it in stone in a way that is impossible with pick and hammer. Fire is, in fact, the only way to attain pure metal.

The gospel that calls each of us into union with God also calls us apart from everything and everyone else. The process of becoming responsible beings leads to wholeness even though it takes us through pain. This refining process fractures even good and loving relationships, such as we know in family, as it prepares us to stand alone before God.

The painful process of individuation is common to human experience and essential to spiritual and social health. This is the process by which we move from unhealthy dependence on associations with and opinions of others as our primary frame of self-definition and self-understanding, to a more balanced definition of who we are and what we shall be.

Most of us are taught from an early age to mediate our sense of self in the midst of others. Obedience to external rules and conformity to external authorities are expected norms. Without such conditioning, neither we nor our parents and teachers could survive. Lack of this conditioning is evident in the breakdown of respect for external authority. Even in circumstances where parental or other familial guidance is lacking, it is exercised by other agents. Gangs and religious cults, for example, become surrogate families and provide external standards by which the individual can define him- or herself.

But most of us desire, and seek to discover and exercise, our particular uniqueness. To do this, we must separate ourselves from those authorities and influences that have shaped our definition of self. This is the pain of adolescence. It is a time and process of growing up, and of growing apart as well.

To what end, however, do we grow up and apart? What is the meaning of this process? Do we grow up and apart in order to exert selfish control over others? Is it for the imposition of my own will and way that I am given my self? Is this process only an exercise in senseless pain without purpose, a punishment upon parents and a tribulation to the community?

Another meaning, however, is offered in the gospels. Each of us is given a unique and individual self. This self is a gift that can be shared with others, offered to the world as a valid and valued contribution to the whole. God, in life, calls us to be separated from our father's body and our mother's womb, to leave our families and the ties of blood and bone that bind us, that we might enter into a radically new kind of family born not of blood but of promise. Life calls us to stand apart from God, the God whose otherness is forever apart from us. We stand apart from God and from one another in order that we may love across the chasm of our difference.

To interpret the experience of individuation in this way redeems the pain of this process. This interpretation expresses what the Christian believes to be God's meaning for this process, or at least to restore to this process a meaning consistent with what we can know and understand of God. Other interpretations may be sensible, may even possess some truth. The interpretation presented here is only a partial perspective on truth—the perspective of one person living in a particular time and place and out of a particular experience. It is a perspective that attempts to make meaning of a gospel that is not peace but conflict. Jesus advocated and encouraged the exploration of such alternative meanings to human experience. That's the trouble with Jesus.

The gospels of Matthew, Mark, and Luke agree that the baptism of Jesus marks the beginning of his vocational ministry. And all agree that the commencement of this ministry was accompanied by the deeply conflicted soul searching that accompanies any difficult decision. This interior process is graphically described in the images of wilderness temptation. The dark exodus of the soul is played out in the dramatic exchange with the antagonist Satan, who offers three tempting alternatives to Jesus (Matthew 4:1-11; Mark 1:12-13; Luke 4:1-13).

At the point of his baptism, Jesus is on the exciting threshold of mature adulthood. He knows and affirms himself with confidence. Self-respect and self-affirmation are powerful forces in our lives. Self-confidence is also seductive. While it is good to have faith and confidence in oneself, this gift that promises so much when offered outward is not without an equally compelling compulsion for a selfish turning inward. The force for giving meets the force for taking. Conflict ensues.

Jesus is tempted first to use his new-found confidence for his own ends. This seduction is made tangible in the suggestion that he satisfy his hunger by turning stones to bread, much as he was later credited with transforming water into wine. (Interestingly, the miracle of providing wine from water at a wedding feast in Cana is, in John's gospel (John 2:1-12), the first public display of Jesus' gifts). The joyful reality of self-confidence comes up hard against the frightening realities of self-preservation and self-'reliance. This conflict is resolved when Jesus dedicates his self-confidence as a gift to God in service to others, relying on God to provide for his needs.

In a second seduction, Jesus is tempted to throw himself from the parapet of the Temple to see whether God does indeed have the power to save, whether the confidence he feels in himself and his God is based in verifiable truth. Like each of us, he wants more than anything else to be able to see for himself that his confidence is grounded in quantifiable reality. The conflict between believing and knowing is resolved when Jesus affirms that each is distinct and that relationship with God is grounded in faith, not knowledge.

In what is counted as the third and final temptation, Jesus is induced to use his self-confidence not as a gift to the world, but as a means for manipulating the world to serve his own ends. Satan's offer to give Jesus everything as far as the eye could see is a vain and presumptuous gesture. There is more at stake than simply the bowing down to or worship of Satan. The promised reward to Jesus is sovereignty, power over everything that he can see. This conflict is resolved when Jesus affirms that everything belongs to God, effectively denying any claim that either Satan or Jesus might make to the contrary.

At this point, says Luke's gospel, the devil had finished and departed. But when Jesus entered his own hometown, he encountered another difficult temptation and conflict flared. Indeed, what Jesus confronted in Nazareth was as powerful a seduction as anything he had faced in his painful introspective wrestling.

When Jesus came before his own family and friends in his hometown, he had every reason to believe he would be understood. They had grown up together. They were steeped in the same ethos, spoke the same language with the same idioms and inflections. But Jesus' expectations came up hard against their expectations, and the conflict was nearly fatal to Jesus. He was more than rejected; he was nearly executed (Luke 44: 14-30).

Why did this episode end so badly? Why was this conflict not resolved more happily? And why did the resolution of this conflict, unlike the three before it in the wilderness, seem not a victory, but a defeat?

Perhaps it was because everyone's expectations were so very different. Each had his or her own notions of what the messiah would be and what the messiah would bring. The people of Nazareth expected the messiah to arise from among them. They expected the messiah to be remarkable in person and demeanor. They may not have known precisely what the messiah would look like, but they were confident they would know the messiah when the time and person came. They expected this person to be remarkable in behavior. They did not know exactly what the messiah would do, but they were confident that whatever this person did would culminate in a new political, social, and economic order that would shift power to them.

Jesus knew this. He could not help but know it. He knew them well, and they knew him. But their expectations were disappointed. They never truly expected a messiah who looked or acted like Jesus. They certainly never expected a messiah whose first priority was not political, or social, or economic, but spiritual.

In this situation, under these circumstances, surely Jesus was tempted—sorely tempted—to succumb to their expectations. Certainly his political instincts were sufficiently astute to encourage tempering his message and his demeanor. With his self-confidence, all he need do was say a few things differently and the people would have been his. Either he would not or he could not meet their expectations.

It is hard to believe that Jesus willfully disappointed people he had so much reason to love and respect. It is equally hard to believe that Jesus lacked the skills to accomplish what they expected of him. But unlike the conflicts of the wilderness temptations, this conflict was not resolved. It was only narrowly averted. Even the conclusion of the episode is strangely inconclusive: "They got up, drove him out of the town, and led him to the brow of the hill on which their town was built, so that they might hurl him off the cliff. But he passed through the midst of them and went on his way" (Luke 4:29-30).

Jesus did not "escape." He did not flee. But neither did the mob relent and disperse. It was a genuine impasse. In this regard, it is one of the most remarkable moments recorded in scripture. In this high conflict, neither violence nor peace results—only an unresolved parting. The trouble with Jesus is that so many of the stories told about him and by him are not neatly resolved, such as the one that follows (Matthew 19:16-22; Mark 10:17-22; Luke 18:18-23).

The man was no doubt sincere as he approached Jesus and asked, "Good Teacher, what must I do to inherit eternal life?" (Mark 10:17-31). This man is sometimes characterized as young, though the gospels give little clue to his age. Of one thing, however, the accounts are sure: this man was rich and powerful.

The young man before Jesus is, in many ways, quite modern. Even his social conditioning seems familiar. Take, for instance, the manner in which he addresses Jesus. "Good Teacher," he calls Jesus. And immediately he is corrected, as Jesus reminds him that to the orthodox Jew, indeed, to all who profess to follow God, none is called "good" save God alone. Evidently this rich young man is a social climber, one who has learned well the art of flattery. But Jesus will not fall for this social ploy. Jesus's reply is a stinging one, and probably causes no little embarrassment. Things are not getting off to a good start.

"What must I do to inherit eternal life?" the man asks, moving abruptly to his reason for approaching Jesus. He does not ask what he must give up, what he must sacrifice, or even what he must pay. He asks what measures he must take to ensure the gift of inheritance. Inheritance is quite possibly the way this young man became rich in the first place.

Inheritance is not usually a reward for something one does, but a benefaction based on and signifying particular relationship. It is commonly the harvest of shared labor and shared love. Inheritance, ideally, has no condition set upon it other than the bond of relationship. The young man has confused the greatest gift of all—the gift of eternal life—with marketplace commodities. He is asking for eternal life, as though he might literally trade and deal with God. Eternal life is but one more possession to add to his collection.

Jesus disappoints the young man by telling him that the gift of eternal life is not something one gets by doing anything. It is not the nature of a gift to be traded, bought, or sold. Gifts of inheritance are given to those who share a particular relationship. So it is not what the man must do, but what the man must be that determines his inheritance.

The young man has kept the Law. No doubt is cast upon his sincerity or his devotion. He has followed the Law to the letter. Interestingly, the portions of the Law Jesus quotes to him are all those commandments addressing family and social relationship. The commandment against murder, the commandments against adultery, stealing, false accusation, and cheating, and the commandment demanding parental respect are all commandments of human social behavior. The young man has kept all these commandments scrupulously. But something is lacking.

The keeping of the Law is of particular importance to us human beings when we attempt to achieve balance between our natural tendencies toward liberalism and freedom on the one hand, and our need for security and order on the other. The real problem was not the young man's money, but his chauvinism, his self-righteousness. He had intentionally or innocently, but certainly erroneously, confused pious and obedient behavior with relationship.

The real sin of the rich young man is revealed straightaway in that subtle, haughty flattery that aimed to set Jesus apart and make him exclusive. I recognize greatness, and goodness, in you, says the rich young man in his flattery, as though to encourage in Jesus a self-importance to match his own. Such flattery was a means by which a rich young man might justify association with Jesus, a man with whom he might not ordinarily be seen in public. The rich young man is patronizing Jesus. Jesus is made acceptable to the young man because the young man could call him good. To relate person to person is beneath him; this has to be a meeting of greatness to greatness.

The impact of the story of this rich young man lies in the

unexpected reply of Jesus, a reply that struck at something far dearer to the young man than his money. The demand to surrender his wealth may not have been as central to the man's concern as the story suggests. For one who was accustomed to keeping the letter of the Law, for one accomplished at doing the external thing perfectly, the giving up of his wealth would have been little price to pay. In every age there have been those of great wealth who have forsaken their money, who have made an art of philanthropic benevolence as the symbol and exercise of their piety, but who have fallen far short of the demand of Jesus. There have been those in every age who have kept the Law to the letter and practiced religion to the point of near perfection, but have failed the greatest test of all. For as they practiced, as they prayed, they exulted in the satisfaction that these actions set them apart from other women and men.

Jesus came to conflict with the rich young man when he told him that to truly inherit, one must be a member of the family. To inherit, one must be son or daughter, one must claim kinship with the entire family of humankind, the entire family of God. One must surrender self-righteousness, setting aside pride in accomplishments and status. One must embrace the reality that all of us are members of the same family. What we do, both good and evil, sets us apart. But what we are, as members of the same family, binds each of us to the other. It is not, Jesus told the man, what we do but who we are as children of the same family that assures inheritance of eternal life.

The rich young man went away crestfallen. The money he would have given up gladly. But the loss of respectability, perfection, and station was simply too much to bear. Responding to the simple demand that he become one with the rest of humanity and embrace kinship with a motley crew of imperfect and sinful people would mean the loss of his exclusivity. He would have done anything to inherit eternal life, so long as he could continue to be that rich young man of distinction.

There were no angry words of condemnation, no ugly explosion. But there was profound conflict without resolution. This clash of expectations, like that discussed earlier, ends in impasse, and Jesus seems content to have it so. That, again, is the trouble with Jesus.

These instances, reported as experiences of Jesus, offer some insight into how he met conflict. At best, they suggest an acceptance of ambiguity, for in neither case is the conflict neatly or conclusively resolved. In the course of his own teaching, Jesus not only accepted the ambiguity of unresolved conflict, he actually cultivated it. The parable is an interesting form. The Greek word *parabole*, meaning "a placing side by side," is actually derived from the more illustrative combination of the prefix *para*, meaning "beside," and *ballein*, meaning "to throw." This parsing of the word better conveys the force of intentionally throwing conflicting images or ideas together, as a parable does. Thus the parable is itself an intentional use of conflict. The craft of a parable consists of skillfully pitting conflicting ideas or images against one another in order to stimulate thought and action.

The parable is further distinguished by the lack of a conclusive resolution. Although some parables in biblical scripture are resolved, some even with a moral boldly stated, such is not the customary form of the parable. Allegories and fables may clearly lead to some conclusive end, but, for the most part, the parable is intentionally ambiguous and open-ended. Therefore, it is now believed that when Jesus told parables, he honored the form and refrained from drawing any conclusions. Where such conclusions appear in the biblical narrative, they were probably added by those telling the story. In some cases, endings may have been crafted only to satisfy the aesthetic or emotional need of the author to see a resolution. In other cases, endings were crafted to enforce a particular point.

The gospel according to Luke actually contains two versions of Jesus' encounter with the rich man, or accounts of two separate episodes of remarkable similarity. One story (Luke 18:18-23) conforms to the preceding story (Mark 10:17-31). But there is another experience with an inquirer who sought information concerning eternal life. In this second instance Jesus is less direct in his reply. In this different version or episode, the person asking the question is not identified as a rich man, but rather as a lawyer. The question, however, is the same: "What must I do to inherit eternal life?" (Luke 10:25 ff).

Jesus asks the lawyer what the Law requires, to which the lawyer replies, "You shall love the Lord your God with all your heart, and with all your soul, and with all your strength, and with all your mind; and your neighbor as yourself." Jesus indicates that this is the proper and traditional answer. But the lawyer seeks more, asking "And who is my neighbor?"

This question opens the door to a new consideration. Certainly there was ample evidence in the scriptural tradition to supply an answer to this question just as the first. The Hebrew scriptures indicate that at various times in Israel's history, *neighbor* was pretty narrowly defined by blood kinship. At other times, the definition of *neighbor* might be extended beyond immediate blood kinship to embrace those who claimed Hebrew ancestry and loyalty to Israel's God. Eventually, the term was broadened further and might include even the stranger. After all, the very life of Israel was dependent on the hospitality of others. So the extension of hospitality to the stranger eventually became an important precept to all Israelites. Once taken in, the stranger enjoyed the status of neighbor. But such liberality did not pertain in all places, at all time, to all people. While Jesus might have referred to specific Hebrew scripture in answer to the lawyer's question, he chose instead to tell a parable.

The parable was about a man who fell among thieves who robbed and beat him, about a priest and a man born to religion who both passed by the battered body, and about a Samaritan who stopped to care for the wounded one. Attention to the rich details of the parable has yielded a bountiful harvest of sermons and lessons on the varied characters and the moral attributes of each. But the character most neglected is the lawyer who put the question to Jesus in the first place. In the end, it is he who is most important to the Gospel narrative, for it is he who represents all who find his inquiry expressive of their own concern.

Like the rich young man, the lawyer is eager to know what, practically, must be done—what hurdles he must leap, what marks he should make, what accomplishments must be tallied—before he can truly live safe and secure. The Law is for him the means to an end, the price to be paid for the attainment of eternal life. For Jesus, however, the Law is the doorway to endless opportunity, the portal to life itself.

The law is obviously too ambiguous for the lawyer. Thus he asks for clarity in the definition of the term *neighbor*. Where, he seems to be asking, am I to draw the limit around my life, and my love? The parable with which Jesus replies is, although straightforward, actually very complex. For in truth, all the characters in the story are, in the most basic sense, neighbors. All four share the same road and the same destination. All trace the same path in the same direction. But for the priest and the Levite, the road is only the means to an end. Each of them skirts the obstacle that would delay and detain, preferring to keep moving toward some higher, more distant goal ahead. But for the kindness of the Samaritan, this road might well have become for a poor wayfaring Jew a literal end in itself.

The priest and the Levite may have had good reasons to move on. Whether they had just come from worship at Jerusalem, or were off to Jericho to fulfill some ritual obligation, the law strictly stated that contact with a corpse would render them defiled. They had no way of knowing the condition of their wounded neighbor. They could not bother risking contact with the battered body of their unconscious countryman. If he was dead, their attentions would either undo what they had already done in the purification of worship, or would hamper them down the road beyond, rendering them unfit to make their sacrifice.

There was risk, too, for the Samaritan. Should he pause by the body, he might be apprehended as the criminal. It was common knowledge that between Jews and Samaritans there was no love. Nor did he have anything to gain, for there was no guarantee of gratitude or reward from this wounded man who, upon reviving, might well be revolted at the sight of his unlikely savior. Instead, the Samaritan spent what must have been nearly the whole day attending to this man, moving him gently to an inn and providing out of his own resources for this stranger's care. Indeed, he went well beyond the minimal requirements of care when he pledged to make good any extra expense that might be incurred. However, it was not just the care and the money that is remarkable; the Samaritan gave up a portion of his life for one who was not only a stranger, but a sworn enemy.

Perhaps because he was a Samaritan it was presumed he had no better place to be and nothing more to do. But this man lost a day's work and a day's income—not to mention what he took from his pocket and pledged against his future earnings—to be with another person. And it was all just a waste of time, really. No Jew would admire him for all his kindness; he was still a Samaritan. Nor would any Samaritan understand or forgive him for reviving one of their enemies. By all accounts, it was a total waste, an act of pure craziness, an example of wild prodigality. And Jesus offers this story as exemplary. Such examples conflict with our notions of fairness, as we see in the next story.

"Take what belongs to you and go; I choose to give to this last the same as I give to you. Am I not allowed to do what I choose with what belongs to me? Or are you envious because I am generous?" (Matthew 20:14-15). These words seem harsh to someone who has labored all day long, only to be compensated at the same rate as a worker who showed up at the last minute. But this is how the hard-working laborer is addressed when he protests a perceived injustice. He is left with a difficult question.

The parable of the laborers in the vineyard is a story of economic inequity. A landowner is seeking laborers to work in his vineyard. He goes out early in the morning and hires one group and sets them to work. Then he goes out at about nine in the morning and finds more willing workers, who are also sent into the fields. The landowner goes on to repeat his hiring forays at noon, three, and even five in the afternoon, sending fresh workers into the fields at each interval. When evening comes and the wages are distributed, the laborer who has toiled since the first and earliest shift is surprised and angry to be compensated exactly as those who have not entered the fields until five in the afternoon.

This conflict touches us at a very tender place since it deals with the monetary worth of human labor. Few companies allow employees to see compensation records, and for good reason. The measure of our worth is so intimately tied, in our minds and hearts, to the amount of our paycheck that such information is detrimental to good relations among any group of workers. Evidently this was as true in the time of Jesus as it is today.

It is difficult to know what prompted Jesus to tell this story, if indeed it is of his own composition. It is actually easier to imagine what this parable might have meant in the time of Matthew's gospel, where it appears. The constant tensions between early Jewish followers of Jesus and their Gentile counterparts frequently flared into conflict. Those who had faithfully "paid their dues" and observed the disciplines of the community were uncomfortable with those who had only lately come into their assemblies. Moreover, when it was suggested that the newcomers might be exempted from traditions that had been observed for centuries, tempers ignited.

The plight of the laborers in the vineyard seems grossly unfair. This parable challenges every notion of labor justice. It flies in the face of basic fairness. It takes precious notions and cherished beliefs and forcefully slams them against a contrasting standard.

The landowner is irrational. What he does is unthinkable. Not only is it unfair to the laborers, it is just plain bad business because it fosters, even incites, employee unrest. But worse, it is horrible economic administration. The landowner pays the laborers who have worked only an hour or two the equivalent of a full day's wage. This fires the expectation of those who have been in the vineyards since dawn's breaking, for they quickly multiply that wage times their accumulated hours of service and imagine a windfall in overtime.

Instead, the landowner pays each the same. He spends far more than is necessary. Indeed, by all modern accounting standards, he cheats himself. Had he imposed a strict hourly rate of compensation, his outlay for labor might well have been less. It is foolish bookkeeping. It is prodigal behavior. Such prodigality is a familiar characteristic of God in Jesus' portrayals. Jesus forcefully juxtaposes human notions of justice with what he perceives to be God's far more prodigal justice. The result is obvious conflict.

That conflict is never resolved in any gospel. Again and again it is made clear that God's ways are not like our ways, despite our unending attempts to fashion God after our own designs. We are never allowed to entertain the possibility that God's ways can be brought into conformity with our own. But neither are we commended in this parable to conform our ways to God's. Instead, we are challenged to deal with our attitude. We are left with the question, "Are you envious?"

What begins as a parable about economic justice brings us, in the end, to the Ten Commandments. We are brought up short by the reminder of how very easy it is to indulge covetousness, to be envious and jealous. To the faithful Jewish believers in the time of Matthew, the point would likely have been painfully clear. And since none of us likes to be brought up short by the truth, their and our response to such a parable is more anger. That's the trouble with Jesus and that's trouble for Jesus. Immediately following this parable in Matthew's gospel, Jesus for the third time foretells his death to his disciples and predicts the conflict that awaits them all as they move toward Jerusalem.

Trouble is just another name for conflict. From the moment he determined to return to Jerusalem, trouble and Jesus went hand in hand. There are few good explanations for Jesus' return to Jerusalem (Matthew 21 ff; Mark 11: 1 ff; Luke 19: 28 ff; John 12: 12 ff). That he was clearly looking for trouble seems the most likely. Even the scriptures themselves support it. At the first mention of his intention to go back to the city, the disciples argued with him. They reminded him that he had only narrowly escaped a stoning when last they had been there. The authorities had made it abundantly clear when they had expelled him that his return would be met with stern action. When he set his sights on Jerusalem, everyone knew he was inviting trouble.

As Jesus sat astride the little donkey, his eyes scanned the crowd. Perhaps he expected to see soldiers, and perhaps they were actually there—they usually were. Surely some of those who caught his eye were there as spies, their street clothes and their common faces the only subterfuge they needed. Everyone knew that no one was to be trusted in a culture where loyalties could be bought for the price of a meal, or less. But troubling as such aspects were, he knew he was deeply in trouble when he saw the palms and the cloaks strewn in his way. This frantic exaltation, and the ferocious expectation behind it, were big trouble indeed. He knew that he could not appease such voracious appetites, and he knew that there would be trouble to pay for that.

The historical roots of the word *trouble* are grounded in older words for "conflict" and "confusion." To state that Jesus was looking for trouble is much different from saying that Jesus was intent upon inciting riot or fomenting rebellion. Those were charges that would be brought against him, as the passion narratives reveal. No, Jesus was looking for trouble in a different way and of a different kind. As he returned to Jerusalem, Jesus made a deliberate entry into the conflict and confusion of his time.

This notion may be far more difficult for us than we can imagine or admit. The very fact that we Christians have ritualized this event may be evidence of our discomfort. Our ritual imposes an order on its original spontaneity and chaotic confusion. And our ritual order imposes an interpretation on the event which steers us safely away from its less comfortable implications for our lives today. Jesus went to Jerusalem to engage conflict, to enter the fray of human life and experience. But what he finds in our churches on Palm Sunday is orderly processions, the poetry of our prayers, the tidiness of our palms, and the rich "Hosannas" of our hymns. All of these things are beautiful. They obscure the frayed and frantic realities that connect our conflicted lives with the lives and conflicts of those streets in Jerusalem.

Why, then, do we hide our trouble? Why do we deny it and pretend it is not here? Why do we persist in the notion that the life of the church is marked by order and harmony? Why do we merely pretend to a unity we are far from achieving, and insist on a peace we cannot maintain? Why do we shy from conflict and make such awkward attempts to mask our confusion? Why do we hide our trouble from the Jesus who is so obviously looking for it?

The church has always been a place of tension and turmoil.

It could not help but be so with so many diversely talented, different-minded people gathered within it. Even the rudiments of politeness are occasionally sidestepped and conflict openly engaged; history certainly bears this out. The church today is in trouble.

And what of our own lives? What of the conflict and confusion that exist among us and within us? What of the many points of disagreement that separate us from one another? What of the confusions that hound and hamper us? Shall we continue to deny them? Shall we continue to dismiss them in silence? Shall we dare to speak up and risk anger? Shall we dare to express our confusion and engage the conflict? Or shall we make a little more trouble? Shall we make a little more trouble and thus make a way for Jesus to find and gain entry into our lives?

Jesus did not have to go to Jerusalem. It was a deliberate choice on his part, and a foolish one by the reckoning of his own friends. Jesus could have remained safely on the margins, tiptoeing gently around the difficulties and the disagreements. He could have preached and prayed in peace. He could have made many people happy and preserved his life to a ripe old age. But Jesus went looking for trouble—and he found it.

Trouble seemed to surround Jesus from the moment he entered Jerusalem; it was never far from his side. Despite the assertion that Judas was a thief, we know that he was loved and respected by Jesus. It seems fairly evident that at their last supper together Judas was seated near Jesus, perhaps even at his left hand. He may have been in the place of honor that others in the room had fought over and sought for themselves.

As for his untrustworthiness, we know that he was entrusted with the financial business of the band of twelve. When it came to faith, Judas was zealous. Also a political zealot, Judas was a scrupulous Jew who showed no little courage in claiming Jesus as his messiah and championing his cause among the Zealot party. He was so single-minded in his determination that he protested vigorously when Jesus' agenda diverted in the least from his expectations.

Thus it was Judas who spoke out when a woman lavished costly oil on Jesus in a ceremony that made Jesus appear more the pampered potentate than the dedicated champion of the beleaguered underclass. But Judas was also human. In the end, his love, his faith, his zeal—his will—conflicted with the will of Jesus. "Do what you must do," Jesus told him in the end.

There was no argument, no defense, no attempt to dissuade. It was a remarkable moment when these two wills—the will of Jesus and the will of Judas—came up hard against one another. Yet Jesus made no attempt to counter the will of the one who opposed him. What is so remarkable is the profound respect that Jesus had for Judas, whose opposition was so obvious, so dangerous. That's the trouble with Jesus.

In his marvelous book, *Blue Highways* (Ballantine Books, 1984), William Least Heat Moon relates his visit with Alice Venable Middleton, a crusty resident of a small island in the Chesapeake Bay. One has to live for a while in that part of the country to appreciate the fierce isolation of such a place. The vulnerability of an island, unprotected from the raw forces of nature that sweep across the face of the Atlantic, is a special kind of fearsome loneliness. The author asks this wise woman, "Tell me what's the hardest thing about living on a small, marshy island in Chesapeake Bay." The woman replies, "I know that and it didn't take sixty-three years to figure it out. Here it is, wrapped up like a parcel. Listen to my sentence. Having the gumption to live different *and* the sense to let everybody else live different. That's the hardest thing, hands down" (page 410).

This was the conflict Jesus engaged in Gethsemane as he looked down a road only he could take. Arrayed on one side was everyone and everything he knew and loved in this life. On the other side stood his dedication to God. It would have been so easy to have gone one way or the other, but in the end he was called to "live different," to chart a new way.

We can guess what his path might have looked like had he chosen to remain with those he loved. He might have taken up their cause, garnered a bit more support, and fomented rebellion; and eventually he would have been put to death anyway. He might have tempered his message, and even abandoned his mission, to live in relative obscurity like many before him and still be accounted a good man.

It is less clear what Jesus' path might have looked like if God had actually granted his prayer for relief. Bodily assumption, a literal ascension, seems the most likely answer. Legends of Elijah's departure in a flaming chariot were still very much alive in his own time. Perhaps Jesus expected, or at least hoped for, such a welcome conveyance as he knelt in Gethsemane considering his options.

In the end, however, he was granted neither. Instead, he resolved to follow his vocation to its conclusion. He would willingly enter the conflict. Note that I did not say "engage" the conflict. There is a distinction.

Jesus is often perceived to have been "passive" throughout the events that followed his arrest. Apart from the final utterances from the cross, we have little evidence of what, if anything, he said to those who were integral to the process that led to his death. Yet his demeanor does bespeak a willing participation; he is neither defensive nor acquiescent. Just as he suggested that his followers be *in* the world, he is *in* the conflict, but not *of* the conflict. He is certainly at the center of the conflict and is, to all appearances, the subject of that conflict. But look again.

Is Jesus really the subject of the conflict, or is he a stand-in? Neither side seems eager to make him the object of their struggle, yet neither can deny the convenience of the role he plays. What makes Jesus so remarkable is, at least in part, that the conflict which ultimately took his life really had so little do with him personally. It is not what Jesus does or does not do, but what he willingly experiences that makes him such a compelling figure.

At one level, the conflict swirling around Jesus is a political conflict between an occupied nation and its imperially imposed government. At another level, the conflict is about differing faith systems. But at a very profound level, the conflict is, ultimately, about the struggle of human will and divine will, or as the biblical traditions have fashioned it, the struggle between life and death. The question at the heart of this conflict is the ultimate question: who is in charge here and who will prevail? Is life ultimately meaningless and limited to sentient human experience? Or is there a greater power, a force for good, whose will for human beings transcends the limits of human mortality?

Jesus does not really answer the questions. Jesus does, however, willingly step into the fray and engage the questions in himself. He is fiercely dedicated to human life and experience. He is equally fierce in his dedication to the God of Israel. Because he will surrender neither, he is literally stretched taut between the two. In the breaking of his life, we can say that he is actually torn by the experience.

It is difficult to know what the first believers actually understood of resurrection when they proclaimed it as the evidence of God's victory in Jesus. As comforting as succeeding generations have found the personal and highly individualized implications of resurrection, it is not apparent that the first believers saw these things so individualistically. Their frame of reference seems to have been oriented more distinctly toward the life of the whole community.

It does seem clear, however, that the testimony of the early community of faith verifies that the passage through conflict leads to new life. When they report Jesus as alive and well in their midst, encouraging them to live without fear, they are affirming that to submit oneself willingly to life's conflict is to advance oneself—and, perhaps, all humankind—in the path toward God. They are encouraged literally to lay down life, to offer themselves, in order that they and others might live.

The trouble with Jesus was—and is—that he stands in the midst of the conflict, allows the conflict actually to live in him even though it tears him apart, in order that new life might be born. The trouble with Jesus was—and is—that he invites us to follow where he has led.

Chapter 3

As It Was in the Beginning

THE FOUR GOSPELS ARE CONFESSIONS OF FAITH REFLECTING THE CONVICTIONS OF AT LEAST FOUR EARLY COMMUNITIES OF CHRISTIAN BELIEVERS. One of the authors, or communities of authorship, provided an extended narrative in the Acts of the Apostles. This document offers some insights into the life of the early Christian community and its formation. The book of Acts shifts the focus away from Jesus to concern itself with what actually happened in the lives of those who followed him.

In some ways their story is almost more fascinating than what precedes it. It is rather easy to understand how and why people might be attracted to the singular charismatic personality of someone like Jesus. What is rarer is the survival of such a community beyond the physical life of the one who was the center, the "glue" that held it all together. The book of the Acts of the Apostles gives us at least one perspective into how and why those early followers survived, even prospered. Through its pages we gain entry into the life of our ancestors and the community that emerged from their shared experience.

One of the first episodes in the Acts of the Apostles is the story of how Matthias was selected to replace Judas among the twelve apostles (Acts 1:12-26). Much about this story is troublesome, not the least of which is the unflattering and unsympathetic portrait of Judas. It conveys a dismissive, uncompassionate, and a very un-Christlike attitude; the scoundrel got what he deserved—plain and simple. Moreover, there is an uncritical commitment to structure and tradition. Citing precedence and justification on the basis of scripture, Peter seizes authority and more or less bullies the group into electing a successor. His primary concern—or rather, the concern of whoever authored this story—is the perpetuation of a structure and a tradition.

This devotion to structure is more than mildly offensive; it is inconsistent with the practice of Jesus. It is particularly repugnant in this context, where one might have expected someone—anyone—to utter a word of forgiveness and to grieve the loss of Judas. There is not the slightest trace that this group saw any connection between the act of Judas and their own complicity in the crucifixion. Jesus contravened tradition and overturned structure, in favor of mercy. Jesus told them throughout his ministry that it was precisely for people like Judas and occasions like the one in which they found themselves that the gospel and its grace were intended.

Then there is the puzzle of Matthias himself—his apparent absence or silence. Where is Matthias? Was he not to be consulted in all this? His election comes quickly, but there is no record of his response, no indication of his willing consent to apostolic work. And what of the ancient method used to determine his selection? It was a gamble. True, the same method had been used to select the kings of Israel. The casting and the drawing of lots were customary means of determining divine will, but was this not superstition? Was this not the kind of divination that Jesus had scorned in favor of the free exercise of will, the free choice offered each of the disciples he had called?

There are many problems with this episode. Yet it reveals our natural human tendencies toward institutionalization and the way institutional structure conflicts with compassion. Nearly every mistake is evident in this passage, nearly every ugliness laid bare. No attempt to dignify or honor them erases the reality. Maybe the point of this story is not the absent, invisible, silent Matthias, but how susceptible we are to the impulse to structure the life of the community.

Still, this attempt at organization failed. It did not hold; else we might have heard more of the ministry of Matthias and of the entire company who remained. Instead, we have only a handful of legends, and most of them unreliable. Indeed, the most visibly influential of all the post resurrection apostles had not yet been converted. Paul would only later emerge as a prominent and forceful apostle.

Still, Matthias haunts this story. The strangely silent figure of mystery touches our history only long enough to tell us that

God's priorities are not tradition and structure. Being the people of God, and disciples of Jesus, is more than ordering our lives according to the patterns and principles of those who have gone before us, more than maintaining those structures they have left in place. Peter's organizational plan failed. Like the Tower of Babel, Peter's plan for order and structure conflicted with and was challenged by the happy confusion of Pentecost, to which Matthias's election serves as prelude.

One warm spring morning I accompanied a group of college students to a large theme park. Before I knew it, we were making our way toward the newest roller coaster in the park, a thing called "The Loch Ness Monster." It all happened so quickly, I am not at all sure how they conned me into it, but very quickly I was strapped in and being hurtled through space. There is one particular spot on the ride that is the closest thing to a free fall I have ever experienced, where one feels as though one is hurtling face-first toward the ground. My whole life flashed before me. Yet before the day was over, I was back on The Loch Ness Monster again. I had become a confirmed roller coaster junkie.

Shortly after moving to Chicago, I discovered another vast theme park and a whole new range of thrilling rides. By then, I had become accustomed to and excited by these twisted piles of tracks. On a recent visit, friends and I mounted the newest and most outrageous ride. When the harness was lowered over my head and locked to the pommel of the saddle under me, I took it all in stride. Then the floor fell away and the cars moved forward, our legs dangling in the air. In seconds we were being tossed around, under, up, down, through, over, and into the air over the landscape of Illinois.

They have misnamed the ride; they call it "Batman." "Ski Lift from Hell" would be far more appropriate. When we stumbled off a short while later, I looked over at a companion and said, "Pentecost is in there somewhere." By the time we finished riding the "Iron Wolf"—a roller coaster one rides standing up (imagine being thrown over a cliff; that is what the first major fall feels like)—then the "Demon" and the "Shock Wave," the kernel of that idea had been knocked loose. When I turned again to the accounts of Pentecost from Acts and from the Gospel of John, the connection finally became clear.

John's Gospel locates the disciples behind locked doors, where, it says, they had placed themselves for fear of the Jews (John 20: 19). While the Acts account neglects that detail, there is some sense that the gathered community of Christ's followers was vulnerable. It is difficult for us to recapture the intensity that attended their meetings in those early years after Jesus' death. But the fear was definitely there, and without it we miss something of Pentecost.

Fear is very much a part of riding roller coasters. In fact, fear is probably ninety-nine percent of the experience. It took me about two seconds to figure that out after I stepped off "The Loch Ness Monster." Something in my knees—or more precisely, the something that wasn't in my knees—told me that what I had just experienced was a fearsome thing. After the pounding of my heart subsided and I could hear and think again, I thought about it.

Theme parks do not spend millions of dollars on machines that are designed to kill their clientele. They want repeat business, not a dead market share. Theme park rides are highly engineered, designed to thrill, not to kill. Indeed, the calculations and calibrations are so very sensitive that I was probably safer on "Batman" than I am on the expressway in my car. So what is it about these rides that makes them so powerful? In my case, it is control. What really terrifies me and many more like me is being out of control. And when I strap myself into a harness and let a machine guided by computer chips throw me around like a limp rag doll, I am definitely out of control.

Try riding a roller coaster sometime without fear. This is difficult, but it can be done. Just strap in, sit back, and relax, like an experienced flier about to be thrust 30,000 feet into space at 400 miles per hour, and let the machine and its operators take over. Those of us who use commercial airlines do that easily enough. The roller coaster will still be an exciting experience, but for entirely different reasons than the sinister. The most exciting thing about such an experience is not that one survives the ride, but that one survives being out of control.

Whether electing a successor to Judas or locked away in fear, the disciples attempted to control their environment, to protect themselves. They were locked away in fear. They feared that the uncontrollable, unpredictable impulses of those outside would overpower them. Yet it was while the disciples were locked away that they report Jesus appeared to them, violating their safe haven and telling them they could not stay there forever.

The story of Pentecost recounted in Acts is even more revealing. In that instance the gathered community lost control of their gospel. The followers of Jesus had no doubt developed a fairly familiar vocabulary for talking about Jesus, and for talking about their faith. As they talked on this occasion, however, the Spirit overtook them. They lost control. They opened their mouths to speak, and the gospel came out. No longer in control, they were speaking of the marvelous acts of God, in languages that were readily understood by the many different people beyond their exclusive company. The truth came out and was made apparent to all around them, even to those they may have feared as enemies.

We too are vulnerable to the Spirit, and that vulnerability scares us. The mystery of Pentecost is a little more accessible to me after my theme park excursions. I wonder whether what the stories are really trying to tell us is that there came a time in the life of the Christian community when they realized that they were no longer in control, nor needed to be. Perhaps they realized, as never before, that they were committed to something far more powerful than themselves, yet skillfully designed and carefully tended by a God who would never let them come to ultimate harm. Perhaps they realized, if only briefly, what it means to trust in God as Jesus had trusted in God.

Shortly after the Pentecost phenomenon, Peter is moved to deliver a brash and headstrong sermon to the gathered onlookers of the event (Acts 2:14 ff). His appeal is said to have added some three thousand newly baptized to the ranks. It is a model to make the modern church envious, for it appeals to our longing to see our cause acknowledged and our churches filled. But it presents one of the most negative examples of evangelism and theology ever written of us. I cannot help but think it was included not as a stimulus to our emulation so much as a caution to our enthusiasms.

The same heedless energy of Peter that marked his time with Jesus has little changed by the time of Pentecost. Heady with the excitement of Pentecost, Peter attempts to counter the claim of some onlookers who have interpreted the event as a drunken melee. Peter confirms that, indeed, there was a kind of drunkenness that besotted the crowd. It was the drunkenness of confidence, the inebriation of joy, and the rush of power that comes of victory and vindication. His mind and heart totally disengaged and his mouth revved into high gear, Peter launches an evangelistic crusade. He begins with an accusation of guilt aimed at pricking the consciences of these bystanders, who are evidently Jews themselves. He succeeds quite handily in his effort and bequeaths to us a tragic precedent of anti-Semitism, for he "cuts them to the heart."

Eight chapters later Peter's angry bravado is shaken (Acts 10: 9 ff). His personal, internal conflict introduces a larger, more public conflict that raged among first-century followers of Jesus, the conflict between Jews and Gentiles.

God speaks to Peter in a dream, lowering a sheet of unclean and forbidden items, inviting him to eat. He resists until he perceives that God is inviting him to reconsider his theological premises and to loosen the taut strictures of his zeal. Peter is moved to confess that God has no favorites. He opens his mind and heart to the possibility that salvation is universally extended, unequivocally offered—that we do not save ourselves but rather we have been saved, and our age redeemed, by the very love of God manifest in Jesus.

The angry, blaming confrontation with the Jews on the fringe of the Pentecost frenzy is incomplete without the later conversion of Peter to a more compassionate and questioning position. As a companion to this episode from Acts, a moment in the Gospel according to John bears closer scrutiny. John's Gospel (20:11-18) recounts that memorable occasion on Easter morning when the resurrected Jesus appears to a weeping Mary Magdalene in the garden, just outside the tomb. Nearly polar opposites, these two episodes—the one from the Johannine Gospel and the other from Acts—stand as reminders of the tension and the task of evangelism.

If Peter's experience reveals the danger of public excess, Mary Magdalene's reminds us of the danger of private reticence. Mary is so consumed with her own grief that she is unmoved by the remarkable presence of two angels. The writer even describes their wardrobe, saying that they were "two angels in white," perhaps heightening the distinctiveness of their being there. Against the gloom of the darkened tomb, their raiment signals that these were not mourners, nor were they likely officials of any kind, their garments appropriate neither to imperial nor ecclesiastical rank and duty.

In a stupor of grief, she barely answers their question and turns away from their attempt to draw her from the depths of her absorption. She turns to find Jesus, but again, fails to recognize him, unmoved by the miracle of his appearing. Mary, who had enjoyed his personal attention, ought to have known him immediately. But even Jesus must call her from her self, grasping hold of her by her name and wrenching her from the depths.

Here, as balance to Peter's enthusiastic extroversion, is Mary's reticent introspection. In contrast to Peter's call to be saved *from* a crooked age, Mary is dispatched *to* a world fraught with the dangers of that crookedness. In contrast to Peter's invitation to the people to gather into a community, Mary is sent out to others. In counterpoise to all the celebrative enthusiasm of Pentecost's public faith stands all the tentative skepticism of Easter's private doubt. And in the two we see the conflicting extremes of evangelism. Whether our approach is to blunder heedlessly and heartlessly, like Peter, or to proceed tentatively with Mary's caution and self-absorption, we find in neither the way. The path, then, is not so clearly marked, but lies somewhere between, in the midst of this conflict.

The third chapter of Acts, recounting the early missionary journeys of Peter and John, tells of a healing credited to them that brings them to the attention of the authorities. "Now when they [the rulers and elders of the Temple] saw the boldness of Peter and John and realized that they were uneducated and ordinary men, they were amazed" (verse 13). It came as a surprise to the rulers and elders of the Temple, this boldness.

For they were unaccustomed to such brash behavior, especially in the common, ordinary people whose deference made and secured these leaders in their lofty positions. It was a challenge to the established order, an affront to authority. So it was that the impact of Easter conflicted with human institutions and attitudes. Alive, dead, or resurrected, Jesus remained a source of conflict.

The rulers and elders may well have been surprised by the boldness of Peter and John when news of their successful ministries were brought forward, but their surprise was as nothing compared with what was to follow. For when confronted by the rulers and elders and questioned, Peter and John spoke clearly to the conflict.

They replied that they were not bound by the authority of the rulers and the elders. Therefore, they would continue to do as they had been doing. They would obey their vocation, speaking, preaching, teaching, healing—living into the resurrection of Jesus. Their boldness that had brought them to court lay not in the beggar's healing, but in their open conflict with authority. After centuries of people doing only as they were told, Peter and John were bold to break the rules and move beyond the threats and tangles of the established order.

It is easy to overlook the specific ministry of Peter and John in their conflict with the rulers and elders. Those leaders were deeply shaken by this confrontation. It may seem they received nothing, those hard-hearted, hard-headed, heavy-handed authoritarians. But something came to the rulers and elders, something they had seldom experienced. In the actions and ministries of these so-called "untrained laymen, they began to wonder," says one translation of the story (Acts 4:13, NEB).

Thus conflict played an important role in the life of the first community of believers, challenging deep-seated assumptions and posing hard questions, not only for those on the outside who were hostile to their faith and life, but also to everything within them that resisted openness to truth and trust.

Despite their wonder, the officials still resolved to squelch the conflict represented by the followers of Jesus. The apostles were brought up on charges of teaching in open defiance of the ban placed on them by the religious authorities. The apostles replied to the charge with a countercharge affixing blame for the death of Jesus upon their antagonists (Acts 5:17-32).

The charges flew on both sides, and the many sad ramifications of those charges through the intervening years are painfully well known. Beyond the lamentable anti-Semitism is a little fragment, all but lost in the argument, which deserves closer attention. "The God of our ancestors raised up Jesus whom you had killed by hanging him on a tree. God exalted him at [God's] right hand as Leader and Savior that he might give repentance to Israel and forgiveness of sins" (verses 30-31). To "give repentance . . . and forgiveness"—that is the matter at hand, a gift of conflict.

The Christian community testifies that forgiveness is a genuine gift of God vouchsafed in the person of Jesus. We may not always understand forgiveness and we may not always appropriate it, but we do acknowledge it. Forgiveness, we know, is a good thing, a desirable thing, even a useful thing. It fits all the qualifications of a gift. We are bold to seek it, frequently express our ardor for it, and are usually happy to get it.

Yet the gift of *repentance*—as distinct from *forgiveness*—is a dubious gift. Unlike forgiveness, repentance is, in our estimation, not a particularly good thing, hardly a desirable thing, and not even a useful thing. We go out of our way to avoid it, frequently circumvent any hint of it, and are profoundly embarrassed to be caught at it. "To err is human," we glibly opine, "and to forgive, divine."

The apostles' accusation was insulting to the authorities. They had no need of forgiveness. There were very good reasons for putting Jesus to death, reasons that are as viable now as in the day they were deployed. Jesus was not crucified, nor the apostles and their successors persecuted, because they were helpless and harmless. They were executed not because of the many wonderful gifts they came to lavish upon seemingly ungrateful people. They were hounded, hunted, and eliminated precisely because they gave gifts that no one wanted. They kept leaving these little bow-tied bombs on doorsteps, and the bombs backfired. I do not want the gift of repentance; I do not want it; I do not need it; it is of no use to me; I have not done anything wrong: this is a prevalent attitude. It is the spirit of our times. We sincerely believe we can do no wrong, and we will go to any length to repudiate anyone who thinks otherwise. It is always someone else's fault, and we'll sue to prove it. Or, if we are feeling particularly magnanimous, we may concede that it is nobody's fault. One does not have to bear the no-fault mentality through the vales of this imperfect world too far before the grim specter of reality arises in the the path and causes one to ask just where all the bad stuff comes from.

It is difficult to embrace the conflicting notion that repentance is a gift. For the Christian, an admission of limitations is not a creed of weakness but a source of great strength. I am frequently wrong. I am certainly wrong far more frequently than I am right. That admission that does not come easily, nor, I confess, does it come any too frequently. But Easter signifies new life emergent from death, including the death of the pretense of personal perfection. From the beginning, then, the community of believers knew that the cost of the gospel was not simply the sword of those who opposed them with temporal authority, but a sword that threatened and sometimes cut through their most cherished personal convictions—and their most virulent suspicions.

The true heroes of history are not always on the expected side. The story of Gamaliel offers a good example (Acts 5:34-42). Gamaliel was a Pharisee of the council "respected by all the people." Peter and others of the apostles had been building a remarkable record of astounding achievements. They had been healing and preaching and, after having been arrested earlier, they had sustained a miraculous deliverance from prison. Word had gotten around, and they had become quite popular with the masses—so popular that officers of the law hesitated to arrest them by force, but compelled them to submit to authority lest the crowds be provoked to violence.

What is to be done about these people? That was the question before the council. And it was within this context that Gamaliel offered advice. His answer was a wonderful testimony to the expanse and prodigality of God's grace and wisdom. Yet the mere fact that it came from the mouth of a Pharisee taints it with suspicion.

It is difficult to accept the possibility that our critics and opponents might occasionally be right. Because Gamaliel was a Pharisee and a member of the council, his advice may have been mere expedience and political posturing. His rationale for the release of Peter and his apostolic companions, because it was given in a political arena, is not appreciated for the profound theology it reflects. To dismiss the Pharisees and their council as merely "politicians," obscures the reality that Gamaliel was also an apostle of God's gospel.

Gamaliel advised to simply let the apostles be. His arguments are buttressed by precedent. He urged careful consideration. Others have come before these men, he said. Theudas had made similar claims and had managed to arouse about four hundred like-minded followers. Perhaps an insurrection had broken out, or an assassin had stepped forward. In any case, Theudas had been killed and his movement quickly dispersed for lack of charismatic leadership. Judas the Galilean likewise was cited as one whose enthusiasms won the affections of a number, but whose subsequent death also quelled the rebels. And to this point, Gamaliel's argument seems one of clever posturing: Just let it alone; don't drag us in.

But Gamaliel reinforced his rationale. "If this plan or this undertaking is of human origin, it will fail; but if it is of God, you will not be able to overthrow them—in that case you might even be found fighting against God!" said the Pharisee.

Gamaliel's position could have cost lives. The episodes with Theudas and Judas had obviously ended in violence. Undoubtedly, Gamaliel's position risked further conflict. To relax control over these apostles and rest confident in God's authority might actually have overturned the very structures of Pharisaism itself. This was the under shadow of Gamaliel's position.

To aver that God is ultimately in charge, and to submit all human activity to that truth, is to make oneself terribly vulnerable. This is why we are so uncomfortable with Gamaliel's advice. We do not want this Pharisee to be right, nor do we want his words to be wise. He is one of the earliest defenders of free speech, freedom of intellectual converse, and freedom of religious conviction, even when all such freedoms challenge his own received orthodoxy. But he distances himself, and distinguishes himself, from his modern counterparts in one regard: he makes his argument not on the basis of civility but of God. He does not advocate that such freedom ought to be safeguarded for the sake of civil order or politeness, but because it is only within such freedom that God's truth can be revealed, and verified, in human experience.

In the example of Gamaliel we are urged toward a new reliance and a new relationship. We are invited to consider the possibility that fighting for truth engages us in the most profound kind of peacemaking, that making the world safe for truth may open us to the most violent kinds of conflict. The position of Gamaliel is hardly spineless, nor is it naively optimistic. People will get hurt, and securities will be overthrown. We are invited by Gamaliel to trust in God—and this from a Pharisee.

Stephen was one of seven people set apart by the early Christian community. His experience of conflict is the first account of martyrdom within the early community of believers (Acts 6 & 7). His death is eloquent testimony to the violence wrought by conflict. Beaten to a bloody, lifeless mass with common rocks, Stephen is victim to unbridled rage provoked to immediate action.

Why was Stephen stoned? "We heard him say that this Jesus of Nazareth will destroy this place and will change the customs that Moses handed on to us" (Acts 6: 14): That was the charge they brought against Stephen. But it was not why they stoned him. The cause of their action was the trumped up charges; according to the narrative, the accusations put forward by false witnesses to buttress the case of the Cyrenians, Alexandrians, Cilicians, and Asians whose anger against Stephen motivated this furor.

When asked to answer his accusers, Stephen certainly did little to avert a confrontation. He made the fatal mistake of quoting their own scriptures back to them, and with a vehemence that grew in pitch as provoking as it was forceful. They unleashed their anger, striking back at this challenge to change, to embrace the change by which justice is done. They fulfilled Stephen's prophecy even as he spoke. It was not Stephen they stoned, but the truth of his words.

The martyrdom of Stephen is a reminder that our traditional response to truth and justice is neither reverent nor respectful, but angry and violent. It is a reminder that few traditions are as old or established as our sinfulness—and the darkly sinful dimensions of tradition. Tradition itself led to the trial and death of Jesus. The traditional human recourse to violence and injustice stoned Stephen.

Yet the author of the Acts of the Apostles adds a cogent detail to the report of Stephen's death that makes this story an important prelude to what follows. "The witnesses laid their coats at the feet of a young man named Saul," says the narrative. The tale of Stephen's fatal confrontation with conflict sets the stage for another story of conflict. In the story of Saul of Tarsus the violent conflict that raged around Stephen becomes a human drama of epic proportions.

Chapter 4
Fear and Trembling

ANANIAS TREMBLED AT THE THOUGHT OF SAUL (Acts 9 ff). What kind of dream was this? Go to Saul? Stand before the man whose very word could issue his death warrant? Why should Ananias go to Saul? Hadn't Saul finally gotten what he deserved? He's blind now, they said, struck by lightning somewhere on the road from Jerusalem to Damascus. What lovely justice! What sweet revenge! Death would have been too easy for the likes of Saul. His life was spared for a world of darkness.

But Ananias could not rest. Something had hold of him. He was deeply conflicted. The voice kept saying, "Go to Saul," but the stubborn will persisted in question and doubt. Ananias wrestled within, not wanting to believe that Saul might be the chosen vessel of God.

Ananias lost. He found himself standing on the threshold, then in the same room with Saul. He rested his trembling hands gently on the despised Saul. From somewhere deep within, the words flowed from Ananias, "Brother Saul, the Lord Jesus, who appeared to you on your way here, has sent me so that you might regain your sight and be filled with the Holy Spirit."

The words permeated the darkness of Saul's world, a deep and suffocating darkness. Whether Saul ever saw or knew Ananias thereafter, we do not know. Saul's ascent from darkness was probably not instantaneous; his descent into the pit had been a slow process made of accumulated wrongdoing. Saul may not have heard Ananias, but he certainly heard God. As he emerged from the darkness, it was as if he entered the world for a second time. When light broke upon his eyes and the birth was complete, he who had fallen face down in the dust of the Damascus road as "Saul," arose to the world as "Paul." Going straightaway to the disciples gathered in

Damascus, and then to the synagogue in that city, the new apostle proclaimed Jesus as the Son of God.

All the world's an Ananias. All who heard Paul were skeptical. Wasn't this Saul, who had created havoc in Jerusalem? Perhaps this was some new trick to ferret out more victims, smoke to drive more of them into his nets. Daily the conflict grew worse. As he preached, tension increased between what Saul had once been and what Paul now was. What use to preach, if none would believe? Was this some special torment, some fresh damnation, designed just for him? What more lonely frustration than to be hated and feared on all sides? He was no longer welcome in the world who knew him as Saul, yet he could find no place in the world as Paul. Then the tide turned violent.

He who had been the hunter became the hunted. There were plots against his life, and he could stay in Damascus no longer. He fled to his past—to Jerusalem. And like Jesus before him, he found danger waiting for him there. Back in the city of Stephen's stoning, the community of believers remembered his name, and they remembered his face.

Then, as enigmatically as Ananias had come forward, Barnabas appeared. Taking Paul in tow, Barnabas led him in among the other believers and spoke to them of Paul's conversion. Barnabas took a tremendous risk, exposing the entire leadership of this fragile community of believers to the eye of him whose hands had nearly destroyed their early attempts to organize. But Barnabas reasoned that it was better to take a chance on a man and lose, than to lose a man for lack of a chance.

From that single act of faith, Barnabas gave the community of believers a powerful shove forward. Paul was mean, irascible, and cunning, but he was also kind, patient, and wise. The same hands that had helped stone the life out of Stephen now laid the very cornerstones of the church.

The story of Ananias, Barnabas, and Paul is a story of conflict and risk. It is a tale of the interior struggles of trust and doubt, and of the outward manifestations of those struggles in intrigue and persecution. It is a story of the ambiguity and paradox woven into the very fabric of the believing community, summarized in a revealing postscript about the church "throughout Judea, Galilee, and Samaria" : "Living in the fear of the Lord and in the comfort of the Holy Spirit, it increased in numbers" (Acts 9:31).

Of Cornelius we know only what is contained in the tenth and eleventh chapters of the Acts of the Apostles. He was a Roman citizen who commanded power and respect as an officer in the military, holding the rank of centurion, one who led a division of one hundred men. His conversion is the first recorded inclusion of a Gentile in the early community of believers, which up to that time consisted solely of Jews.

The tale of Cornelius and Peter and the visions or dreams issuing from their relationship remains intriguing. In this relationship between an untutored fisherman and a Roman military officer we find a paradigm for life in the midst of conflict. In their dreams these two disparate men hear the voice of God, a voice whose words bring them and bind them to each other. This powerful experience and the relationship of these men influenced the witness of Peter to the first council of the church in Jerusalem, a witness that resulted in the opening of the believers' community to those outside Judaism.

Just days before meeting Cornelius, Peter had had a puzzling vision. While he was at his noon prayers, he grew hungry. Waiting for his lunch to be prepared, his mind wandered, as minds swayed by hunger are wont to do. In his dream Peter saw a great cloth lowered from the skies, a vast and varied picnic spread within its folds. The menu contained all manner of food forbidden by Jewish law. Three times the vast banquet was lowered before him, and thrice he was commanded by a voice to kill and eat of the forbidden bounty. And three times Peter denied, the second threefold denial recorded of him—a nice detail that lends symmetry and credibility to the story.

In the conflict between obedience to the law and obedience to the voice, we see the struggle of one challenged to change. It is the tension of one being challenged to venture in faith. Perhaps it was the triple denial that most moved Peter to a change of heart. It is interesting that in all three denials of the mysterious voice, Peter responds "No, Lord," clearly indicating that this is no demon come to taunt him, but the voice of God, urging him to move beyond the rigid confines of ritual law.

"At that very moment," says Peter, "three men, sent to me from Caesarea, arrived at the house in which we were. The Spirit told me to go with them and not to make a distinction between them and us" (Acts 11:11-12). Thus it was that Peter moved beyond his resistance and, following the footsteps of his forebear Abraham, stepped into the path of faith that led him to the house of Cornelius the centurion.

There Peter met one who was as hard for him to accept as anyone could imagine. Cornelius was in all outward appearance a man the same as Peter. But he was also a Roman citizen, a centurion—a military man—a man to be feared and even hated by the Jews among whom Peter numbered himself. Here was this stranger, this Gentile, relating to Peter how God had appeared to him and had commanded him to summon Peter, to hear the gospel, and to be saved.

Surely the tension between Peter and Cornelius was palpable. It was the confrontation of opposites across the chasm of difference. On each side, long-held beliefs and sacred values were challenged and the relationship of the entire human family hung in the balance. But in the resolution between Peter and Cornelius, relationship took precedence over regulation.

Peter was not asked to convert the entire Gentile populace, only to go to Cornelius. There, in the presence of his Roman enemy, that unclean outsider, Peter stood. In time, Peter would stand in the midst of his Jewish critics. When that time came, he would cite the visit to Cornelius and his Gentile household, and he would tell them a story of forbidden food, of a command to eat, of a threefold denial, and a change of heart. He would speak only of what he knew, and offer his own simple conclusion, asking, "Who was I that I could hinder God?" (Acts 11:17).

In years to come, when he would relate the story of his meeting with Cornelius the centurion in Caesarea, Peter proclaimed that only one other occasion had so moved his life and shaped his faith, and that was the day of Pentecost itself.

James and his brother John, sons of Zebedee and early companions to Jesus, seem always to have sought first place. Or perhaps it was their mother; she exhibited the worst attributes of the pushy parent when she came to Jesus and in the presence of her sons, begged that Jesus give them preference (Matthew 20:20-28). There is no indication that either of them was the least embarrassed by this brazen request.

"Sons of Thunder," they were called (Mark 3:17). The nickname implies that James and his brother John were pretty loud and probably obnoxious, but may also reflect their zeal. That would explain their affinity with Peter, whose company they often shared. The three of the them must have been quite a handful.

Since they seem to have been close companions of Jesus, one wonders just how meek and mild Jesus really was. It is doubtful that a milquetoast would attract such blustering rowdies. The four of them—Jesus, Peter, James, and John—seem a rather formidable quartet, impressive and maybe even intimidating.

James was the first of the apostolic community to be martyred (Acts 12:1-5). His death is not without irony. This boisterous, pushy, selfish bully wanted to be first. He achieved his goal—not, perhaps, in the way he and intended, but by being the first of the lot to lose his life for his associations with and loyalties to Jesus.

In his zeal and loudness, James probably invited Herod Agrippa's fury. Those qualities we deem detriments—the pushiness, the loudness—were actually the energies and gifts that led the post resurrection community out of grief and mourning and propelled it into the world. The community of believers in Jesus didn't just fade away, as the authorities had hoped it would. A few of its members—like James—continued to be visible and vocal. They were either politically stupid or blindly courageous, or both. They moved freely about, and they would not shut up. They persisted in conflict until the axe of the empire severed their heads, attempting to silence forever, but instead making martyrs—and an angry determination that only kept the story alive.

James was not reluctant to assert himself. He reminds us that conflict was actually the force that gave the community of believers their life, the engine that drove them forward and carried them and their story further than even they could imagine.

Barnabas was one of those most remarkable people who balance ability with humility. What they accomplish far overshadows their recognition. Barnabas was one of the greatest, arguably *the* greatest of the early apostles. It was Barnabas who nurtured the faith of Paul and introduced the former zealot and persecutor to the wary community of early apostles and believers. Paul had no place within the community until Barnabas established it for him.

Barnabas, in his senior capacity as apostle to Antioch, called Paul to be his assistant (Acts 11:25). From that point onward, the two worked side by side, cultivating the church. It was they who began to welcome into the early church the non-Jewish converts and ultimately found themselves the center of controversy at the first council of the church, convened in Jerusalem to deal with the controversy of Gentile inclusion.

It was in Antioch among those who observed the work of Barnabas and Paul that the name "Christian" first attached to the community of those who believed in Jesus (Acts 11:26). But of the things written of Barnabas, one reference to him stands above all the rest: "For he was a good man, full of the Holy Spirit and of faith" (Acts 11:24).

"He was a good man." There is no catalog of his many accomplishments or his deeds. In this respect, Barnabas is the model apostle, the one Paul might emulate but would never fully duplicate. Nor would Barnabas likely have expected or desired imitation from his assistant and colleague. For Barnabas was apparently one of those rare persons whose ministry is most remarkable for what it enabled and encouraged in others.

There is no long and exhaustive record of deeds attached to his name. It is not that he was not admired; he was imposing and august. In Lystra, where Paul and Barnabas were involved in the healing of a man who was crippled, the people took them as gods. Paul they called Hermes, but Barnabas was to them as the greater deity, Zeus (Acts 14:8-13).

The goodness of Barnabas was that he was a person animated by the spirit of relationship with God. He did what he did, seeking no reward or gain—indeed, he never received any wage from the church he served, but rather lived off his own labor apart from his ministry. He did what he did, it seems, because it was something he loved doing, a tangible expression of the pleasure he derived from his relationship to God.

That he was a man of faith was evidenced in his confident conviction. That he was sometimes embroiled in controversy for what he did is evidence that he was concerned more that the right and good thing be done, rather than whether it be judged proper and acceptable by others. There was nothing more important to him than God and God's family. He did what he deemed best, and he accepted the consequences, which were often far-reaching. Eventually Barnabas had to answer to the larger community of believers. That community that had only lately earned the name "Christian" was about to mount its first institutional convention, and the work of Barnabas would have a prominent place on the agenda.

Seldom have two men seemed so different as James and his brother, Jesus. James seems to have been a serious boy, devoted and faithful to his Jewish heritage. In some respects, he was more like his cousin John the Baptizer than like Jesus. James was given to asceticism. He never drank wine outside the rituals of faith, nor did he partake of meat. Beside Jesus, he seems sober and conservative.

Jesus was reputed, by his detractors, to be a notorious lush and a wastrel. He broke bread and joked and traveled with a rough lot, many of them socially unstable and most all of them poor. He dined with Gentiles and was friendly with women, treating them as equals. Rigorous distinctions meant little to him. He must have been a constant embarrassment and irritation to James. Like many brothers before and since, their lives clashed hard against each other in constant contrast and conflict. They went their separate ways, each probably thinking the other a bit mad. Jesus may have been frustrated that James could not shake loose from his long-held traditions, while James despaired over the extravagances of Jesus, who claimed to see beyond this world to another, and saw this world so much differently from other people.

It is easy to imagine the scene: James standing in the midst of the assembly, all of them looking to him as their leader, their bishop (Acts 15 ff). The arguments had been long and bitter. The Judaizers wanted circumcision required of the Gentiles, and they were insistent. The law was still the law, and better in the eyes of God to be scrupulous than to abrogate it entirely. Surely the zealous James would understand and support their position, opposing Paul, Barnabas, Peter, and all whose enthusiasms claimed no other authority than their personal experience. James would have the last word. Even Barnabas and Paul waited in silence for his decision.

James strained to remember the words, repeating them with care in a voice heavy with the weight of responsibility. Reciting the prophet, he said, "After this I will return, and I will rebuild the dwelling of David, which has fallen; from its ruins I will rebuild it, and I will set it up, so that all other peoples may seek the Lord—even all the Gentiles over whom my name has been called. Thus says the Lord, who has been making these things known from long ago" (Acts 15:16-17).

The silence was filled with expectation until he resumed. Accepting the responsibility for leadership, he rendered his opinion, saying, "Therefore I have reached the decision that we should not trouble those Gentiles who are turning to God" (15:19).

James made the decision. He rendered a verdict, and it became the accepted practice, shaping for all time the institution of which he was head. In that moment, James revealed himself to be the genuine brother of Jesus. The teaching of Jesus, as he related his own perceptions of God, and the direction of James, as he rendered his opinion in the assembly, were both clear examples of bold and decisive action based on the authority of human reason informed, but not restricted, by scripture and tradition.

The liberating witness of James was his determination to act decisively as a responsible creature. His witness reminds us that we are to value our own experience and reason. Those who denied the authority of Jesus did so on the basis of his humanness (Matthew 13:54-58). Because he was one of them, they discredited his witness. What they revealed was not simply their mistrust of Jesus, but their own lack of respect for themselves. Because Jesus was no different from them, his word could have no value, his witness no authority.

Yet it was in that very humanness that some, like James, realized the sanctity of human responsibility. As creatures of God we are endowed with responsibility, the ability to respond in faith and hope and love to the life and the world God gives us. In Jesus, whom we believe to be the full incarnation of all that God desires of humankind, we see the high regard of God for the human race, a regard far higher than that revealed in the response of the townspeople of Nazareth.

When James was called upon to arbitrate the dispute that divided the community, he could have avoided conflict. He could have tabled the issue for further study. He could have deferred to one side or the other. But taking into account the traditions of both sides, he called them to a radical departure that set them on a new course. He acted upon no other authority than his own reason, informed by tradition and shaped by scripture, and advocated a new way.

I wonder if James, as he pondered the moment, recalled the day the people had rejected his brother in Nazareth. They had rejected the authority of Jesus partly because James was his very human brother, because such literal familiarity undermined their confidence. As Jesus is said to have remarked, "No prophet is accepted in the prophet's hometown" (Luke 4:24). Now, in Jerusalem, James' word was respected because Jesus was his brother. It was an irony too sad to be savored.

The sixteenth chapter of Acts begins with the story of Paul and Timothy. Paul has traveled to Derbe and to Lystra, where he has met Timothy. Timothy was a relatively young man, certainly younger than Paul. But Timothy was already a disciple of Jesus, a believer in the Christian gospel. Timothy's mother was Jewish, yet also a believer of the gospel. But Timothy's father was a Greek. Thus Timothy was reared in a household that represented in microcosm the larger situation of the early church.

At Paul's direction, Timothy is circumcised—not a small sacrifice for an adult convert. The action is undertaken not for ritualistic purity, but for clearly political reasons. The council in Jerusalem had already determined that Timothy's Gentile heritage would pose no obstacle to his faith.

But Paul and Timothy would be conducting their ministry in other places. They were to visit Lystra and Iconium, where they would be bearing word of the council's decision to open the household of Christianity to all people. They would be inviting Jewish believers to a faith shared with Gentile converts. And they would be inviting Gentiles to a religion previously hedged by Jewish custom and community. To bear such authoritative word, the messengers would need impeccable credentials; thus Timothy was circumcised. Among Jews his advocacy for the uncircumcised could not then be dismissed as self-serving. Among the Gentiles the measure of his devotion was rendered irrefutable.

Paul and Timothy set out on their mission and immediately met with success. The churches, "were strengthened in the faith and increased in numbers daily" (Acts 16:5). "They went through the region of Phrygia and Galatia, having been forbidden by the Holy Spirit to speak the word in Asia. When they had come opposite Mysia, they attempted to go into Bithynia, but the Spirit of Jesus did not allow them; so, passing by Mysia, they went down to Troas. During the night Paul had a vision: there stood a man of Macedonia pleading with him and saying, 'Come over to Macedonia and help us.' When he had seen the vision, [they] immediately tried to cross over to Macedonia, being convinced that God had called [them] to proclaim the good news to them" (Acts 16: 6-10).

How did they know that Asia was forbidden their preaching? It would seem they found out the hard way. They went through Phrygia and Galatia, but were prevented from speaking the word. Whatever frustrated their designs, we are not likely to know. But where they might have said some rather nasty things about those who frustrated and restrained them, they chose to interpret this setback as God's doing.

Similarly, they were thwarted at Bithynia and Mysia. There they were not even allowed into the region, but proceeded directly to Troas. It seems a devastating outcome, especially in light of all the trouble Timothy had been put to in preparation for the journey. There is no good reason that Paul and Timothy should not have been utterly embittered by these circumstances. Yet they persevered; their experiences were ordered by God.

When at last they did meet with success it was in Macedonia, and the aftermath of a dream. Paul had a vision, dreaming that a Macedonian had come to him seeking their help. Macedonia was not to prove a windfall harvest. Paul and Timothy did, indeed, finally meet someone who would listen—but it was a woman named Lydia who, along with a handful of other women, was their only audience. Lydia and her household were baptized—not a great showing for such a portentous dream. But it was enough to encourage them. As Paul moved around Macedonia, his companions increased. His actions provoked attention and shortly thereafter, Paul and Silas were thrown into prison.

Evangelism is fraught with conflict. It is difficult to give witness to faith, especially in territories that are hostile and to people who are uninterested. The greatest frustration, however, is that evangelism is made to seem so easy by those who advocate it so heartily. The inference is that those who find it difficult are either lacking in talent or will, are either stupid or lazy—or worse, unfaithful to the gospel.

This episode from Acts suggests that certain frustrations are not indicators of failure, but of limits—and those are not the same thing. In evangelism, as in all else, we are God's partners. When we do not succeed in the clear articulation of the gospel either in word or in deed, it is not a judgment of our fitness. Neither is it a judgment of the fitness and worth of the other person—the object of our efforts—that connection and communion is not made.

From Paul and Timothy we learn to trust our vision but not to insist on its every detail. Paul dreamed of a man of Macedonia, a welcome sight in the nocturnal ramblings of a frustrated apostle. He dreamed too of the conversion of a nation but had to make do with the conversion of a woman and her family. Yet he did not carp about the scale of his mission, nor complain that it seemed so little for so much. His impulse to go to Macedonia was correct, though his mission there had to be tailored considerably to meet the moment with grace.

For intensity of emotion and fervor of feeling, there is no conflict to equal the family fight. That is what made the situation in Thessalonica such a volatile one. It was there that Paul and Silas encountered a scene that was to become a sad commonplace in the life of the Christian community (Acts 17:1-15).

The argument that ensued and the hostilities it engendered all took place within the synagogue. The first schism of the church was not the division of the Eastern from the Western church. The first, and for that reason the most tragic, separation was the rancorous division that separated the Jew from the Christian.

Part of the blame, the part for which Christians must account, lies with Paul. The record is embarrassingly accurate when it says quite plainly that Paul "argued" with those in the synagogue (Acts 17:2). That was his first mistake. He was, after all, only human. Once the argument began, the point would be a long time lost.

The combative and competitive nature of argument caused sides to form, and those present aligned themselves accordingly. From that day on, the energies of each group would be devoted almost entirely to the defense of its argument and justification of the division, which is the exact opposite of the ministry of reconciliation that was preached and valued by Jesus.

The tragedy of Paul's argument in Thessalonica, and of all arguments subsequent to it, lies in the important distinction between rightness and righteousness. God nowhere demands that we be right, that we be correct. But everywhere, and always, God desires that we be whole, which is the meaning of the word *righteous*. To "be perfect" (Matthew 5:48) as God is perfect means to possess an integrity as comprehensive as God's—to be able not only to discern truth and judge without error, but also to forgive and love without condition. Such wholeness may be beyond our achieving, but not beyond our aspiring. Salvation, then, is not a matter of correct theology or superior argument. Salvation is a matter of community, of love between people of differing opinions and respect between people who are as varied as snowflakes. Such love is hard work, fraught with fear and trembling.

The conflict of Thessalonica was followed by a visit to Athens, where Paul seems to have grown considerably. He proves more than merely tolerant when he stands before the

Areopagus and addresses those gathered there. "Athenians," says Paul, "I see how extremely religious you are in every way. For as I went through the city and looked carefully at the objects of your worship, I found among them an altar with the inscription, 'To an unknown god.' What therefore you worship as unknown, this I proclaim to you" (Acts 17:22-23).

This congregation is unlike the congregations Paul had addressed in the synagogues; he is now far from his Jewish roots, wandering in alien territory. Yet he recognizes and is sensitive to the faith of the Athenians. He pays homage to their faithfulness, praising them for the considerable gifts of their own religious heritage. He makes no attempt to destroy their faith, nor even to raise up a rival god to their own. He does not deny or denigrate their conviction or their religion. He does not begin by telling the Greeks they are wrong, or stupid, or infidels.

This was a major turning point, but a temporary relief. After Athens, Paul was subjected to a steady diet of conflict. He would know only brief respite from the strife. In and out of court, in and out of jail, his work continued.

Paul seemed to make a career of being on trial, and quite a fine one, at that. He had a knack for handling himself under pressure, and he grew more adept with experience. On one occasion (Acts 22:22 ff) he was brought before the Roman tribune. Clearly, Paul was the one on trial. But when the meeting ended, called to a halt by the Roman officials who feared for their prisoner and likely their property as well, the tables had turned. Paul had learned how to use his Roman citizenship and his Jewish heritage to advantage.

When, shortly thereafter, he was handed over to the chief priests and the Council (Acts 22:30 ff) , he was no less skillful. Using his knowledge of the theological divisions that separated Pharisees from Sadducees, he had only to inflame the old wounds and conflict became his friend. His accusers fell into the heated arguments of their parties. Their violence was a credible and tangible witness that even they themselves could not agree sufficiently to bring the case against Paul.

One can certainly look upon such episodes with grave suspicion; one can wonder just what Paul's cleverness was intended to do or reveal, and whether in fact it was not a manipulative and self-serving gesture. But one also has to admire the political acumen exhibited when the unified case his detractors sought was foiled by their own disunity. All Paul had to do was claim certain allegiances, and human nature and partisan politics did the rest.

What the religious officials wanted the Roman officials to believe was that they had a holy and unified case against Paul, that theirs was a righteous and moral case of profound religious dimensions. What Paul revealed is that the religious officials were far from convincing, wildly divided, and zealous in their party loyalties to the extent of violence. Paul revealed that they were humans, and fairly base humans at that.

Paul demonstrated the dichotomy between a verbal and an incarnational witness. That truth is quite easily revealed. All one has to do is walk into any of the councils gathered to consider the relevant issues of our day and claim allegiance to one or the other side. That will suffice to set the tigers loose and, given sufficient rein, they will claw one another to bloody shreds in the name of all that is holy.

The struggle of the church, from its inception, is the struggle evidenced by Paul amid the conflicts that brought him to trial. It is the conflict between a faith proclaimed,which is only ideology, and a faith lived, which is true incarnation. As Paul evidenced, when words fail to speak this truth, or power conspires to silence it, conflict itself will proclaim it.

In the story of Paul's many trials, there is one instance in which his safety was guaranteed neither by his own Christian community nor by the Jewish community of his birth, but by the Roman government (Acts 25:13-21). The frailty of the tiny Christian community was not sufficient to sustain Paul's well-being and the factionalism of the Jewish community posed the most dangerous threat to his safety. A plot had been fomented against his life. He could not be sent in safety to Jerusalem, not because he would not get a fair hearing there—though that is almost a certainty—but because there were zealous opponents who had vowed to fast from food and drink until he was assassinated.

The Roman authorities who respected Paul's birthright as a Roman citizen, determined to ensure him a fair trial. Indeed, he languished in prison for years, ostensibly because the Roman officials wished to keep peace with the Jewish authorities. But Festus, who had inherited this controversial case from his predecessor, Felix, brought the case before King Agrippa for advice and counsel. Festus wanted to dispatch the case and to do justice, but he could not appeal the case to Caesar without a clear charge. So the wheels of Roman bureaucratic justice and the formidable military power of the empire protected Christianity's most potent leader. Prison became the first seminary, and the capitol city of the empire became an unseemly see. Politics became an incubator, and the structures of government the midwife, of this emerging faith.

In the strange economy of God, those institutions and communities we regard with skepticism and hostility are sometimes beneficial for us, even as Rome was for Paul. Such stories encourage us to be dubious, unsettled in our judgments, opened by doubt to unusual perspectives and unique opportunities. They remind us that our easy assumption that the world and its politics are always and everywhere at odds with God's will, is challenged in the experience of Paul, who used those politics and their structures to decidedly creative, and holy, ends.

Such doubt is a healthy antidote to all that closes us off. To be dubious is, in a very special way, to be faithful. To be dubious is to be open to the workings and the will of God everywhere, in everyone, and at every time. To be dubious is to be armed with that due caution and care that allows for the possibility of God's good in unlikely places.

As the book of the Acts of the Apostles draws to its end, we find Paul in the custody of a Roman soldier (Acts 28:16 ff). Paul's case has been remanded to the judgment of the empire. But the imperial authorities see no case for death, so Paul is kept in custody. He is free to teach and work, supporting himself at his own expense. The Roman guard accompanies Paul not so much to hinder or survey his freedom, as to protect him from those who wish his death.

Paul summons the Jewish leaders of the Roman community. It is not they but their counterparts in Jerusalem whose accusations have landed him in Rome. Paul meets with the Jewish leaders of Rome, and they seem most accommodating. They have received no word from Jerusalem concerning Paul, so they are open to hear his story and urge him to tell it. They seem most generous and gracious. They do admit that they have heard many ill reports of the newly emerging sect that Paul advocates. But, again, they seem quite fair minded as they invite Paul to share his witness. They want to know of Christianity, so new it does not yet bear that name universally.

Paul did share his witness, and, according to the text, there were some among these leaders who came to believe in the gospel. Yet there were also those who did not agree. As they departed Paul's company, the apostle is reported to have quoted them a passage from the prophet Isaiah:

> You will indeed listen, but never understand,
>> and you will indeed look, but never perceive.
> For this people's heart has grown dull,
>> and their ears are hard of hearing,
>> and they have shut their eyes;
>> so that they might not look with their eyes,
>> and listen with their ears,
>> and understand with their heart and turn—
>> and I would heal them.   (Acts 28:26-27)

To this passage, Paul adds his own admonition, saying, "Let it be known to you then that this salvation of God has been sent to the Gentiles; they will listen" (verse 28).

So the generosity of the leaders is repaid with what seems indignation at their disagreement and the threat that what they have rejected will be given to others. It seems an odd place to conclude the first narrative history of our community, but this may be a most appropriate ending, too. For when we turn to the Gospel of John, we encounter a similarly perplexing, and distressing, conclusion.

The ending of John's Gospel, like all that precedes it, must be read with extreme caution. This account (John 21: 20 ff) is the product not of a single author, but of an entire community whose primary identity and political loyalty are centered on the person of one named the "beloved disciple," believed to have been John. The fourth Gospel ends with Peter in conversation with Jesus, and John just behind them. If one substitutes for the individual apostles in this story the very communities that sprang from their witness, the picture takes a different shape.

Imagine the community of Peter's followers, perhaps gathered in Rome, represented in the figure of Peter. Like members of every such community since, they consider themselves to be on intimate speaking terms with Jesus himself as, indeed, Peter is in this vignette. But just beyond is the community of the beloved disciple, the followers of John, the disciple who leaned upon Jesus' breast and asked at the last supper just who it was that would betray Jesus—an episode replicated in this little tableau. Thus the Gospel of John ends with a nasty jibe directed by one community of believers at another of the same family.

The community of the beloved disciple is here reminding the community dedicated to Peter's memory that it was the beloved John who sat at the favored place at table, and it was Peter who betrayed Jesus in denial. In the narrative Peter asks about the lingering John—what about him, what of his future? Jesus replies that it is none of Peter's concern. So what if John should remain until Jesus return?

To communities awaiting the imminent return of Jesus as they struggled against oppression and persecution to maintain their own lives, this strange reference cuts immediately to the core of this enigmatic passage. This story reveals one community's bare jealousy of the other. The community of the beloved disciple, the followers of John, are saying to the followers of Peter: If you are wondering about our tenacity, our perseverance, and just where we stand in the larger scheme of things, know that every time you look over your shoulder, we shall be here—even until the return of Jesus. At the end of the four Gospel accounts, and at the end of Acts, we are brought face to face with human jealousy and institutional factionalism.

Interestingly (perhaps providentially), it is these two texts that are appointed in the lectionary for Saturday in the seventh, and final, week of Eastertide. The great fifty days of Easter reaches day forty-nine and finds us at one another's throats. With brutal realism, the church comes literally to the eve of Pentecost not in glory but in shame. On the eve of this great day, the church of Acts is left with Paul spitefully taunting those kindly Jews whose only offense has been to disagree with him and, in the Gospel of John, with two noble communities of our ancestors arrayed against each other. Not a very nice picture.

It seems a strange place to situate the church at the end of Eastertide, on the eve of Pentecost—a deliciously ironic posture for the reception of the Holy Spirit. For those in pain and grief over their divisive jealousies, a surprise is in the offing. Likewise, for those who find smug security and jealous joy in their distinctive separations, a surprise lies ahead. For God will not leave things as they are nor allow the divisions to stand. The Holy Spirit will alight upon all and, with maddening, loving prodigality, ignite this tinderbox. Conflict will become conflagration. And all, in every sense, will be burned up and blown away.

Chapter 5
We've Always Done It This Way

THE GOSPELS AND THE BOOK OF ACTS REFLECT THE GENESIS OF THE CHURCH. Within the first generation after the death of Jesus, those who knew Jesus and had come to know of him gathered to make some meaning of what they had experienced in their close associations with him and the lasting influence of this experience within their lives. This happened in several different places, among several different groups of people, as we can see in the four different Gospel accounts.

As these communities matured, they discovered each other. Obviously, what they held in common was their experience of Jesus, either directly or through stories of those who had known him. But they also learned of their differences. As relationships and communications connected them, they found cause and occasion to share what they held in common and debate what they didn't. When it was to their advantage, which was certainly true in times of persecution, the various communities probably cooperated. When persecution was less a threat and the luxury of independence presented itself, they went their separate ways. But as their lives unfolded, they became better organized and structured.

We can see this development in the Gospel texts themselves. In Matthew, for example, we see the early struggle to discern and define the meaning of Jesus within the framework of Judaism—and all the tension that provoked. The Luke narrative seems in many regards less contentious and certainly more artistic, suggesting that it was written from the relative security of privilege—or at the least, peaceful coexistence with the forces of religious and political imperialism that made life so difficult for other communities. The Johannine account, being the latest, reflects a developed theology heavily influenced by the Greek philosophy with which it is in conversation. It also reflects, in its claims for its own authority, a sense of its own distinction and its own orthodoxy and the contention this produced in its relations with other bodies of Christians. The book of the Revelation, which seems to have been produced by the same community, is much more difficult to place within this extended meditation. But at the very least, it reflects a time in the life of that community when it felt itself very much under siege. The conflict it addresses, relying heavily on a coded language of numbers, visions, and images, was a severe persecution, probably the violent and brutal war waged against the Christians by the Emperor Domitian in A.D. 95.

The Acts of the Apostles details the early missionary activity that went into the making of the church. But it is the collection of letters attributed to the early missionaries themselves that remains one of our richest legacies. Like all letters, they are topical. They were originally intended to address specific congregations or individuals. Their references to the life and difficulties, the successes and problems known to each person or congregation, are interesting and instructive. Indeed, that is probably why they were selected for inclusion in the canon. No doubt, other such documents were generated, but only these few were chosen.

They remain, most likely, because they reflect common experience. A letter written to one congregation was sometimes shared with another. While the exact issue addressed in the letter to the first congregation may have been different from the concerns of the second congregation, they were sufficiently akin to make the general principles articulated in the letter applicable, and useful, to both. Sometimes minor changes were made in the text to strengthen a point or to relate the letter to a particular place and time. But the letters proved instructive and were included in the canon of scripture, in large part, because the issues they touch upon and the principles they articulate are timeless.

In the course of ministry, I hear many stories. Some are offered by individuals who use their stories as a way of either sharing excitement or discerning the way through difficulty. Others are the stories of groups, congregations, who are also eager to share their accomplishments or to resolve their dilemmas. In every case, the first and most important question I ask myself is: Where have I heard this story before?

I'd like to take you on a tour of a church.

In this church there are those who find charismatic leadership a source of strength; they follow in admiration, and those whom they follow encourage them, heedless of the factions that emerge.

Others in this church find their strength in a rigid adherence to the traditions of the past. They are fond of the way things have been done and are accustomed to certain ways. They know and enjoy the company of each other, but have lately begun to feel that they are being ignored or outnumbered by those who consider them to be behind the times.

Some in this church like the gospel they have heard, especially the proclamations of new life and the freedom that accompany it. But they are divided in their notions of how this gospel is to be lived practically. One side defends more relaxed sexual standards. The other side advocates an ascetic sexuality, one bounded by greater self-discipline.

There are women in this church who find the traditional male chauvinism of their culture oppressive. They, too, have heard the gospel and have heard within it a new and exciting word of liberation.

This church numbers among its members some who are unabashed Pentecostalists. They actually speak and pray aloud in tongues, much to the consternation of those who find such behavior in worship a distraction, or worse. Moreover, some of the Pentecostalists demand that baptism in the Holy Spirit be recognized as the true mark of faith.

In this church there are those, bless their hearts, who have just tired of it all. All the wrangling and in-fighting have taken a toll. They have all but given up on spirituality. They don't know what to believe anymore. Faced with the chaos and confusion of the present, they are content with a simple, yet materialistic belief—indeed, a hope—that death will at least provide an end to the strife and that heaven will at least be a rest from it all.

Sound familiar? It should. It's a pretty good description of what any neophyte investigator would find after poking around in most any church today. But the church I have described isn't here or now. It is, in fact, the community of Christians gathered in first-century Corinth.

Paul, in a letter to that congregation, condemns its sinful divisions. It is not the disagreement, but the division—the tragic separation—that is for him the most serious transgression in the catalog of Corinthian craziness.

Paul was disturbed, and rightfully so, about reports that reached him concerning the divisions of the congregation meeting in the home of Chloe (1 Corinthians 1:1-17). Quarrels had broken out among the believers, and the congregation had fractured into cliques. Some claimed loyalty to Paul. Others claimed allegiance to Cephas, others to Apollos. Even those who claimed to be "Christ's own" were guilty of the same petty factionalism represented in the other little groups.

Factionalism seems built into the fabric of human experience and human institutions. We live by particular denominational identifications, the products of the charismatic influence of pioneers in the faith. Our appreciation for the faith of people like Cranmer, the Wesleys, Calvin, Luther, the Continental reformers, or the choir of saints of the Roman or Eastern tradition, all contribute to our distinctive faith. In our different traditions, respect for, admiration of, and allegiance to modern pioneers distinguish the particularities of our separate confessions. And the choice of particular heroes or heroines signifies our place on the complicated political spectrum within our communion.

We take pride in these distinctions, and we express that pride in many ways. We can be haughty when we consider ourselves somehow superior for having found a better way. We can be disdainful of those who have chosen to follow a course different from our own. We spend the better part of our energy and our evangel simply justifying to ourselves and others the rightness of our particular faith claims.

Concern for the state of the church should draw us with peculiar interest toward Paul's amazing statement that Jesus did not send him to baptize, but to proclaim the gospel. Did Paul misstep in this statement that sounds suspiciously heretical and

certainly anti-establishment? Is Paul contradicting the commission of Jesus to go into all the world and baptize in the
name of the trinitarian God, or is he revealing his understanding of the Christian gospel? When Paul says that his ministry
and ours is not to baptize but to proclaim the gospel, and to do
it without the language of worldly wisdom, he is telling us that
winner-take-all argumentation and semantic debate are not the
way of Christ. Parceling the family into parties, of whatever
stripe or persuasion—even of baptized and non baptized—is
itself anti-Christlike.

Paul, then, is in conflict. He is not at odds with the factions;
he is at odds with the factionalism. He believes that God has
endowed the human being with the ability to transcend the factionalism and to live in harmony, even without compromising
the differences represented in the factions.

"And so, brothers and sisters, I could not speak to you as
spiritual people, but rather . . . as infants in Christ. I fed you
with milk, not solid food, for you were not ready for solid food.
Even now you are still not ready" (1 Corinthians 3:1-2).

With that caustic reprimand, Paul confronted the congregation at Corinth. Their malady was smallness, not insufficiency
in numbers; indeed, they were probably a fairly large congregation. The smallness was not in the membership; theirs was an
attitudinal smallness. They were infants in Christ, and, like an
infant, they were absorbed with themselves. They were self-cen-
tered. Their vision was protracted. What was of importance to
them was of little importance to the rest of the world, or so they
thought. Their partiality, their strife, their shameful shenani-
gans were nobody's business but their own.

But Paul knew otherwise. Paul knew that what they did
among themselves and within their culture would convey, even
more strongly than their words, the truth of who and what they
were. Maturity was their most powerful ministry. So long as
they remained bickering infants, they failed to communicate
the gospel.

The world in these waning days of the twentieth century is
literally reeling from wave after wave of change. The fall of the

Berlin wall, the disintegration of the Soviet Union and Eastern Europe, and reform in South Africa are probably only the beginning of profound change. Reform such as we see within the Soviet states, Eastern Europe, and South Africa depends on far more than structural change at the top.

In one news account, a woman of East Germany saw beyond the euphoria of those celebrating atop the crumbling concrete wall dividing Berlin. She was sober, and not a little sad, as she reflected that exciting as the moment was, it remained to be seen whether those who had for so long lived without freedoms would be able to assume the responsibilities they must now take up.

Responsibility, or rather the lack of it, lay at the root of Paul's anger and frustration with the community at Corinth. What most distressed him was the unwillingness of the Corinthian Christians to assume responsibility for their own faith. They had, instead, ceded their responsibility. What faith they owned was not yet their own, but was Paul's or belonged to Cephas or Apollos. Their partisan identifications of themselves were an abdication of personal responsibility, an unwillingness to confess a faith of their own. They were content to believe not in God, but in Paul, Cephas, and Apollos and in what Paul, Cephas, and Apollos believed. Paul called them infants— dependent children—because they were unwilling to proclaim a faith of their own.

Any and every witness to an incarnational faith must enflesh that of which it dares to speak. It is this integrity of word and substance that the woman in the shadow of Berlin's wall so wisely questioned. The word of freedom cannot be separated from the work of freedom. True freedom depends upon the integration of word and work—integrity of word and deed.

Evangelism, indeed good news of any kind, is communicated by integrity. Integrity is the soul of righteousness. Righteousness is not a matter of being right or being wrong, but of being responsible, of bearing responsibility for what one is, for good or for ill. The exhilaration at the tumbling of the Berlin wall, the suspense attendant to the Soviet upheaval, the drama of South Africa's bid for change are only tentative words of hope. Beyond each of these events the more difficult and decisive work is yet to be done, when each citizen in each land takes personal responsibility for justice, bears personal responsibility for freedom, weds the promise with practice in integrity.

The same may be said of our witness of God's truth, and the faith that is in us. Such witness, and the evangel it proclaims, will be neither decided nor delivered in our adherence to one party or another, nor in our fidelity to one doctrine or another. It will not be decided by our sacramental submission to the rites of Baptism, or any of our outward expressions of conviction and promise. Our most potent witness will be —as it has always been—genuinely incarnational, bearing the Word in the substance of our persons. It will consist in being persons of integrity and, subsequently, being a people of integrity.

"I don't know how anyone could be so damned stupid." The words were heavy with frustration. We had been hammering away at the mysteries of trigonometry for hours, but I was no closer to understanding the complexities, much less the way to the solution of the problem. My dad, an engineer who designed computerized systems that literally traced the heavens and measured the depths of the seas, was struggling to help me, his eighteen-year-old son, grasp the rudiments of math. It was like using a jackhammer to remove a nut meat. Those teen years were turbulent enough. Then trigonometry tipped the delicate balance. The tension between father and son reached a crescendo when my dad slammed the book down and berated me with impatient disdain. He did have the good sense to leave the room.

Against this memory consider the dietary argument in Corinth (1 Corinthians 8:1-13). The question arose concerning the eating of meat that had been dedicated to idols. The more literate and intellectual parties in the dispute believed that God cared little about dietary matters. God was more concerned about the contents of their hearts than the contents of their stomachs. But there was another, more literal group in that community who believed, with equal sincerity, that dietary laws were a necessary discipline. When Paul spoke to the issue, the real problem he addressed was not dietary at all. What concerned him most was the arrogance that threatened to splinter the community.

The intellectuals could not understand how anyone could be so stupid as to take the dietary injunctions literally. Their vantage points, perspectives, and experiences separated those factions from each other like my father's advanced years, considerable experience, and academic degrees in engineering separated him from my youth, inexperience, and ignorance. Between us stood our pride, arrogance of unimaginable proportions.

The goodness of deep conviction is always relative. Those who have supposedly known best have led us into some of the worst human disasters. Those who know best invade other countries and impose governments and practice a condescending parentalism. That is the sad history of imperialism, under whatever banner. Those who know best insist upon only one expression of religious faith, or recognize the efficacy of only one style of prayer, or the validity of only a particular baptism and creed. Those who take a more moderate position, who embrace the middle way as the best, have too often stood by in arrogance and apathy and let the divisions grow all the wider.

Paul confronted the people of Corinth with an appeal addressed to the rightness of neither side, but to the arrogance of both. Paul maintained that quite apart from the question of who knows best, those who know Christ know that love, not knowledge, is the strength of community. When knowledge separates, divides and wounds, it is no longer right, nor good, nor of Christ. Even the most correct knowledge cannot justify or save those who torment and shatter our world.

My father has often said that the more he learns, the more he realizes how little he knows. The morning after our blowup he came to me with an apology. No problem, nor answer, was worth the loss of our relationship. Humility restored what pride had threatened to take from us. And the lesson was one of far-reaching effect. Not many years later Dad left his career in engineering to become a teacher of math and physics—a teacher respected and beloved by his students for his patience and his generosity.

What God revealed to the world in Jesus, and Paul to the Corinthians, my own father revealed to me. It is not rightness to which we are called, but to righteousness. It is not correctness to which we are called, but to courage. And we do not need answers half so much as we need each other.

The matter of resurrection seems always to have been a breeding ground for conflict. Some in Corinth were not wholly comfortable with the concept of resurrection (1 Corinthians 15:12-20). Some maintained that there is no resurrection of the dead. They might concede that Jesus was resurrected, but they definitely concluded and were teaching that there was no hope for the rest of us. And for this skepticism, Paul took them to task.

"If there is no resurrection of the dead, then Christ has not been raised; and if Christ has not been raised, then our proclamation has been in vain and your faith has been in vain. We are even found to be misrepresenting God, because we testified of God that [God] raised Christ—whom [God] did not raise if it is true that the dead are not raised. For if the dead are not raised, then Christ has not been raised. If Christ has not been raised, your faith is futile" (1 Corinthians 15:13-17a).

Paul concluded with the captivating suggestion that "If for this life only we have hoped in Christ, we are of all people most to be pitied" (verse 19). Or, as another translation renders it, "If our hope in Christ is good for this life only and no more, then we deserve more pity than anyone else in the world."

Those in Corinth who denied resurrection are not identified, nor are their motives made plain, but one can surmise. What was to be gained by such denial? If there is no resurrection for anyone, then we ought to take maximum advantage of such life as we have. Eat, drink, and be merry, for tomorrow we die—this advice strikes a chord of recognition. After all, from what we can see of experience, life is indeed fleeting; and the more we see of it, the more quickly it flees.

But the motto of the believing Christian is really no different from that of the hedonist. The faithful Christian also believes that we should eat, that we should drink, and that we should be merry today because, in truth, tomorrow we most assuredly will die. So the difference between the Christian and the hedonist is not in the motto. The difference is in the resurrection. For what one believes of resurrection determines not *whether* life is to be celebrated, but *how* life is to be celebrated. And therein lies a profound difference.

Belief in resurrection is frequently denied or denigrated as a form of deferred gratification: "Pie in the sky by and by." But Christianity does not advocate that we defer enjoyment of this life for the attainment of some future blessedness. We do not suffer in this life in order that we might find blessedness hereafter. The peace and happiness of life in God is fully realized in our experiences of this life, even in those experiences deemed painful. The overwhelming reality evidenced in Jesus is that our life and God's life are not separated and compartmentalized, but are unified and inseparable. Thus Paul insists that to deny our own resurrection is automatically to deny the resurrection of Jesus as well. Consistently, to deny the resurrection of Jesus is to deny our own resurrection.

To believe in resurrection—Jesus' and our own—is to affirm a continuity of life that is frankly unattractive to a good many of us. Most of us have no trouble with the notion of living forever. The vast majority of us in this American culture presume as much every day and spend a good bit of time, energy, and money on that presumption. What is more bothersome is the responsibility of resurrection. If there is no life beyond this one, if I am not accountable beyond death, if everything ends with my final breath, then it matters little how I live this life. To live as if there is no tomorrow is to live heedless of consequence.

A human being with no sense of or appreciation for resurrection, a human being with no faith in resurrection, is as dangerous as an armed adolescent in a street gang. The most dangerous person on the street is not the hardened and experienced criminal, but the youth with a loaded gun—a person with no sense of tomorrow, no sense of consequence. Hence the urgency and the frustration with which Paul greeted this news from Corinth. Paul believed in resurrection, not for what it promises of the future, but for what it contributes to the present. Participation in the Resurrection begins here and now— and shapes the here and now.

I met a remarkable woman when we were both undergraduates, she at one college and I at another. We met the summer following my freshman year and remained friends thereafter. Julie was bright, marvelously funny, and outrageously outspoken.

In the late 1960s when Julie and I were collegians, American universities were only beginning to experiment with housing men and women in the same buildings, even on the same halls. Julie's campus was ahead of my own and had introduced coed housing some years earlier. She lived in a coed dorm, and I asked her how the residents dealt with the inevitable question of sexual intimacies. Her reply was characteristically funny and predictably bawdy (slightly altered here). Without blinking an eye, she replied, "When you have to face them over the oatmeal the next morning, you don't mess around the night before."

Paul would certainly have enjoyed her comeback. It would have made a nice retort to the Corinthians arrayed against him on the other side of the resurrection argument. The prospect of everlasting relationship might significantly alter our present relationships.

The church in Corinth was not the only congregation with troubles. Indeed, there is a depressing sameness in the conflicts that emerged among the early believers. The issue of Gentile inclusion was certainly widespread and occupied much energy. Paul struggled with this tension in Ephesus. That church, like several others, was locked in combat over the issue of circumcision (Ephesians 2:11-22).

Paul urged the opponents to work at life together, saying that such walls as divide—in their case the walls of traditional, historic Hebrew ritual that divided the culture into Jew and Gentile—are walls that Jesus had broken down. Jesus had broken down those walls, said Paul, in Jesus' own flesh and blood. For Paul, the church was the incarnation of Christ's body broken.

Paul maintained that through the broken body of Jesus a new humanity emerged and became the community of the Christ. It was a community reconciled, but it was not a community homogenized. The Jewish adherent to Christianity still bore the marks of circumcision in the flesh, and the Gentile still bore the evidence of Gentile origin in the intact foreskin. Each remained distinctly different. And it would be the hallmark of the community of the Christ that such difference would forever mark its life.

This image of division haunts the church. It is the image of the eucharistic sacrament. Yet the church resists. The ideal community, according to the prevailing definition, is a group of like-minded people representing organic and institutional unity. The basis for community—the common bond that holds people together—is, at best, any agenda promising common benefit. Shared self-interest, common gain, is the adhesive of most human community.

The community is a repository of tradition and a haven of security. A community of salvation, by extension, is a community promising safety and security. The community saves us from having to relate to and live with difference, saves us from having to give up whatever it is we deem necessary to our security. Struggling to secure this vision, we see it fragment again and again.

Fragmentation is the very image of sin. Division is an expression of our weakness. Because we fail to build unity into a massive organic whole, we have failed in our mission. But have we?

As he matured in his faith, Paul saw fragmentation creatively. Fragmentation could be God's gift to the church, even God's will for the church. After all, in the broken body of Jesus the two very different peoples—Gentile and Jew—found a way to be together in their differences. Could it be that the very Spirit of God spoils our designs for homogenization in order to build the church of God's own vision?

Our vision of the church is limited. It is an image made of walls. It is a vision built of our own prejudices and our own concerns. For the Jewish convert to Christianity in Ephesus, the mark of the church was the mark of circumcision shared all around, and for the Gentile, just the opposite. The church remains a distinct and identifiable temple to sameness. That is to say, the church is not open to travel, nor even to hospitality. The church is an established respository that neither moves nor welcomes difference. No matter how noble our cause or lofty our vision, in the end, we envision a church of oneness, and that is quite a different thing from a church of unity.

The mark of God's church is fragmentation, the eucharistic

mark of brokenness. We are the body of Christ, and our ministry ought to look like him. For the sake of unity and for the making of a new humanity, this body—the church—may find its ministry in a rending that forever breaks down walls and rips the Temple veil.

The unity God seeks and the new humanity God is making demand a place where all sorts and conditions can meet and be reconciled. To be that place, in this world, we shall have to be broken. We shall have to be torn from the idols of our own ideals. Our orthodoxy will be ruined, and our purity will be sullied. The stones of our walls of division, the rocks with which we have routed the sinner from our midst, will be reduced to sand. The banquets we have made of our resources and by which we have fed ourselves to fatness will be reduced to crumbs. And not to decide may be the hardest decision of all.

The good news, then, may be that those energies we have given for so long to the vain dream of building sanctuaries of sameness may now be given to meeting one another in all our myriad differentness, where we may know the Christ, who "came and proclaimed peace to [those] who were far off and peace to those who were near; for through him both of us have access in one Spirit to [God]" (Ephesians 2:17-18).

Willpower and discipline are not the same thing, though a culture that diets compulsively, jogs religiously, and works obsessively is confused on this issue. Discipline is less an action or activity than it is an attitude. "Those who live on the level of our lower nature," says Paul to the Romans, "have their outlook formed by it, and that spells death; but those who live on the level of the spirit have the spiritual outlook, and that is life and peace" (Romans 8:5, NEB).

That "spiritual outlook" is the foundation of Christian discipline. It is neither will nor work, but attitude that makes the disciple. That may be why dilettantes are more common than disciples. A dilettante is one who cultivates an interest in a subject rather as a pastime or a hobby, one who dabbles, often rather superficially, in a subject. The civil dilettante wants the rights of democracy without any of the responsibilities of democracy. The religious dilettante wants the esthetic trappings of the faith without any of the hard work of the faith.

This tendency is hard to combat, as history and experience teach. When Paul speaks to the Romans about their life as disciples, he tells them that discipline is not a matter of strict adherence to the law. In fact, he confesses to them his own difficulty in keeping the laws of God. He tells them that his own willpower is insufficient to meet the demands of the law. And he tells them that despite the most egregious transgressions of the law, there is no condemnation for those who are united with Christ (Romans 7:14-8:4). That is not to say that there is no law, but rather to say that discipleship rests upon a different attitude, one that sees law as a means to an end and not as an end in itself.

When Paul speaks of those who live on the level of our lower nature, he is not speaking of those who give themselves over to all manner of bad behavior. He is speaking of those who live by selfish and self-absorbed human willpower. He is speaking of all who continue to believe that discipline and discipleship consist of exerting one's mind and talents to the achievement of one's own will. He is speaking of those who believe that discipline and discipleship are measured by our ability to exert our own will, our ability to control ourselves and the world around us. When Paul speaks of a spiritual outlook, he indicates that discipleship and discipline begin in a new attitude.

Some of the hardest work done all week is, or should be, done in church—in our worship. These are not occasions to stop growing or to stop working, but to be reminded that we were not made to exert our power over this world, but rather to join our wills with God's will as partners in creation. It is our work to turn this world over and over in our hands to see the many different ways that God brings beauty and mystery to life within it, and to find the places where our hands and hearts are needed to fulfill God's work. We are not gathered to see our design, but God's.

To be a disciple and to exercise that discipline is not, then, to gain mastery over the material, but to place oneself in service to it. It is not to shape the world to our own liking or build it after our own image; it is to practice looking at the world and one another in a new way. It is to practice looking at the world and one another as God looks at us. This is what truly distinguishes Christians: that we are not here to fulfill our own wills, but God's will. That's truly a distinctive attitude in this world. And it's a difficult discipline to maintain, as Paul readily admitted.

It is a difficult and demanding discipline to see the world and all that is in it not as a stage for our power, but as the studio of God's creativity. It is difficult to see one another not as meat to be managed, marketed, and manipulated, but as the material of God's imaginative and artful creation.

It is difficult to get beyond selfish notions of the gospel. It is difficult to lay aside arguments about race, gender, sexuality, and the host of other matters that consume so much attention. The point is not so much that these things ought not matter but, rather, that what matters in these arguments is not what we argue about.

We approach these issues with little or no concern for the other person, but only with our own fears and attitudes boldly exposed. We are not nearly so concerned to find a place in our hearts for the pain of the outsider as we are to scream and yell about our own discomfort and inconvenience at having to deal with outsiders. We are not nearly so concerned to find a constructive purpose in the gift of each other's differentness as we are to insist upon the value of our sameness. We are not nearly so concerned to open ourselves to new challenges as we are to seal ourselves behind fortresses of fear, which are, of course, no real defense against the changes God demands of us.

These arguments spill over into our civic debates. In the arguments over the place of different races, ethnicities, genders, and sexualities in our culture, we are not nearly so concerned to make room for others as we are to safeguard what little room we have carved out for ourselves. We are not nearly so excited by the creative possibilities of our diversity as we are fearful of the perceived dangers of our differentness.

Thus it ought not to be any surprise to us that we live in such fearful, fearsome, destructive, and depressing times. The reason may be that we embrace a hostile attitude and enjoy only a dilettante's interest. It may be that there is no easy way out, and that life demands very hard work from us. But also, sadly, the reason may be that we refuse to work hard for anyone or anything except ourselves.

The gospel imperative and invitation to take up the yoke of Christ is deceptive (Matthew 11:28-30). This passage is sweet enough. It sounds so peaceful and comforting. But in truth it is hard to see any good news in this invitation. Jesus invites all those whose work is hard and whose labor is heavy to a very strange notion of comfort: He offers one yoke for another.

He does not say work will cease, neither does he say that there is no burden. The gospel is at least realistic, and Jesus is honest. Jesus, and the gospel he proclaims, acknowledge that the discipline of faith and the discipline of freedom are work, very hard work. Jesus does not say that we shall cease from our work. He says only that our attitudes will change.

The church bequeathed by the earliest believers was in many ways different from its modern successor. But we are joined by a shared faith and by those basic human aspirations that attend our life. Therefore, the tether that draws us together is common faith in God as manifest in Jesus and the common institution that grew out of that faith. That common faith and its institutions share a vision of Christ's lordship over all the earth and an image of the church as the vast kingdom of the saved, the faithful and loving remnant of God's chosen people.

In his first letter to the Corinthians, Paul confronted a community of believers grown smug in their own righteousness. Confident in their status as a community beloved of God, they must have been surprised by some of what Paul had to say to them. It is true, said Paul, that Christ has brought all to life and thus brings this life to God. It is true that the Christ is destined to reign until all enemies be put to subjection beneath his feet. But it is also true, says Paul, that the Son himself "will also be made subordinate to God who made all things subject to him, and thus God will be all in all" (1 Corinthians 15:28, NEB). Paul strikes at the certainty of the Christian church that sets itself up not as a means to an end, but as an end in itself.

The reign of Jesus was never intended to last forever, nor was faith invested in Jesus to be confused with faith in God. The reign of Jesus was to be a reign of reconciliation. The kingdom belongs not to Jesus but to God, the maker of all things.

These are surprising words, even shocking and heretical. They throw us off balance. They conflict with our deepest convictions about ourselves and our institution, the church. If they succeed in surprising us, they leave us no longer quite so certain of what is good and what is evil, what is saved and what is damned. This may not be so great a loss as some fear. To come to a wondering and searching means that we have come back to where we belong. If we can no longer be certain of our own judgments, we might more fully rely on God's judgments. If we can no longer discern between those in our society who are good and those who are evil, then we must treat all alike.

If we do not feel that we can entrust our lives fully to the institutions of this earth, including the institution of the church, then we might find that elusive reign and realm of God that catches us off our guard and pops up at the most interesting places and times. If we are no longer certain of anything, but are like the blindfolded child in the midst of a vast parlor game, we may enter more fully into the spirit of that party which is our life. If we are no longer filled with certitude, we might be filled with surprise.

When all the lights of our own brilliance are dimmed and darkness encompasses us, we are the more susceptible to that piercing light that took Paul, takes the world, and redeems all—by surprise.

Chapter 6
The Truth Will Make You...Anxious

A S WE HAVE SEEN IN PREVIOUS CHAPTERS, ISSUES OF INCLUSION WERE PRESENT FROM THE EARLIEST MOMENTS OF THE CHURCH'S LIFE. Jesus, in his own lifetime, was charged with indiscriminate behavior in his open acceptance of diversity. Some criticized him for associating with the poor and outcast. Less frequently noted, but probably just as often, he was criticized by his poorer adherents for associating with the rich. His open acceptance of people without regard for the customary standards of social status was consistent with his affirmation of a God whose self-expression is manifestly prodigal.

The abundant prodigality of God figured prominently in Jesus' teaching on creation and forgiveness. According to Jesus, God gives abundantly and God receives freely. The parable of the prodigal son (Luke 15:11-32) is the most familiar example. In this tale, one of two sons goes to his father and demands his inheritance. The father complies with the request. The son spends his money lavishly, ending in poverty. Ashamed to go home to his father and brother, he holds out as long as he can. When he can no longer stand his outcast state, he returns home, ready to confess his mistake.

But before he can confess, the wayward son is greeted by his father, who is ecstatic at the son's return. Despite the fortune he has already given the son, and lost, the father produces new clothes, rings, and other gifts. Calling for a lavish banquet, the father celebrates the return of the wastrel son.

Such behavior makes no sense to the brother who has remained faithfully at home. He is angry and jealous of his brother's treatment and considers it a grave injustice against himself. When he complains to their father, the steadfast son is not affirmed in his jealousy. Instead, the father reaffirms his love of both sons, and he also claims his right to be as generous as he pleases. In the end, it is the faithful son who is revealed to be the greater wastrel, for in hoarding his affection for his profligate brother, he is wasting the precious gift of love and kinship. In this regard, the faithful son represents one face of human nature's wastefulness, just as his spendthrift brother represents another.

Moreover, it is the father who is revealed to be the true prodigal. For in the eyes of both sons the father's generosity is a surprise. It is totally unexpected, as the sons' reactions reveal. The wastrel son, creeping home empty-handed, certainly does not expect to be welcomed, much less celebrated. The steadfast son is equally taken aback by the extravagant outpouring of love and money at his brother's homecoming.

Therefore, both Jesus and the God he preached and incarnated impress the world with their prodigality. Such generosity of giving and such generosity of welcome reception is alien to common human nature and experience.

The prodigality of Jesus and his gospel was the source of much conflict. In his associations with a wide variety of people, in his travels into and through alien territory, in his blatant disregard for the political, social, religious, and economic structures that ordered life in his own time, Jesus came up hard against opposition. He challenged established truth, not by negating that truth but by introducing an alternative truth.

The possibility of multiple truths challenges the logic that there can be only one truth, one ultimate reality. The conflict of multiple truths begins for most of us even before we learn to speak. It begins at birth, when we are separated from our mothers' bodies. For a little while, connected by our dependency on her breast, we literally get our first taste of difference at weaning. It's all downhill from there. Despite the hovering dotage of admiring spectators around the crib, we gradually learn that we are not the only creature in the universe. The conflict of multiple truths begins when the truth of my existence collides with the truth of your existence.

This process continues throughout our lives. It extends beyond our individual experience to the experience of groups. It extends beyond the experience of groups to the experience of nations, and beyond nations to a planet, and beyond one planet to a universe. The process extends backward in time, as our

ancestral stories of Creation suggest. This is the truth of
Genesis. The process extends forward in time, despite all our
best efforts to control it. This is the truth of the resurrection life,
life that is not even bounded or controlled by death. But most
important, the process engages us here and now, demanding
our constant attention. This is the truth of the gospel of God
manifested in Jesus, and a two-edged sword it is.

The good news is that we have God and we have each other.
The bad news is that we have God and we have each other. No
wonder we are anxious, troubled, and distressed.

The challenge of difference and the conflict it generates, like
the two-edged sword, can cut in different directions. At certain
points in my own life, difference has been a welcome friend.
This was especially true when I reached that point in life when
one begins to embrace that prickly but delicious reality of one's
own difference: the teen years.

As mentioned earlier, I grew up in the rural South. My family was active in the Methodist Church. We attended every
Sunday. My parents were involved lay leaders. I attended
Sunday School, vacation Bible school, sang in choirs, played the
piano and organ for worship, and was a leader in the Methodist
Youth Fellowship. Ours was a fairly homogeneous community, and our congregation reflected that homogeneity. Most were
farmers or commuters to good jobs in neighboring cities, but
solidly middle class in income and outlook. As an involved
member of the congregation, I was exposed very early to the
underside of life in community; I was well aware of the conflicts
that simmered and sometimes raged.

While I was still in high school, I grew weary of the fighting
in church. I found it inconsistent with the precepts I had
soaked up from Sunday school and a lifetime of sermons (evidently gained as much by osmosis as by listening). I answered
a local newspaper classified ad seeking an accompanist for a
church choir. It seemed the answer to a prayer. I needed a job
and income, and this job provided a logical excuse for leaving
my home church.

I was hired and left my church and denomination to work
for a congregation of very poor people. Most of them were

laborers in the local textile mills and furniture factories, and some were transients who landed in this run-down urban mission, literally on the wrong side of the tracks in a town where tracks really were a social boundary. This was an entirely different congregation of very different people in an entirely different community.

What a difference it would make, I thought. And for a while it did. But in time the differences gradually faded and I learned that my new church community, although composed of different people, exhibited many of the same conflicts I had known in my old church community. I was really rather glad when I was accepted at a university too far away to continue my job with this congregation. I was ready for a break from church.

Once I arrived on campus, I was immediately caught up in the challenge of difference. Suddenly I was actually living with people who were not my family in a dorm that was not my home. Everything was different overnight. I was a day person; my roommate was a night person. I preferred to study in my room; nearly everyone else preferred to study in the library, or not at all. Classes did not even faintly resemble what I had known in high school. Nothing was quite as I had once believed it to be.

When I was ready to go to church, I looked around. Having been active in the inner workings of congregations my whole life, I wanted only to sit in a pew and to experience church from a different perspective. I visited several congregations before I wandered into the local Episcopal church one Sunday. It was quiet, and its stately gothic architecture, so different from the modest scale of churches I had previously known, seemed appropriate to my religious sense. People were pleasant enough, but no one spoke to me, and I loved them for that. I took my place in a pew and looked through the service bulletin, preparing myself. (As a child, I had occasionally attended Catholic mass with my paternal grandmother. The sight of people respectfully genuflecting on their way into the pew, or kneeling quietly in prayer during the organ prelude, appealed to me.) When the organ and choir combined in the resounding music of the opening hymn, and a vested crucifer, torchbearers, choir, and clergy moved with dignity down the aisle, I knew I had found what I had been seeking.

I stayed for four years. I loved the Book of Common Prayer and the Hymnal 1940. I was at worship nearly every Sunday. Three or four Sundays each month I prayed and sang the canticles of Morning Prayer in the congregation. On the first Sunday of every month we shared communion. But I was never involved in the life of the congregation. Though I was faithful in worship, I was not confirmed and made it a point not to be active at all in the programs designed specifically for students. In time, however, I became very much involved in the life of the Episcopal church. In the last semester of my senior year of college I was confirmed, and that same autumn I entered an Episcopal seminary. The challenges started all over again.

When I arrived at seminary in the fall of 1970 I encountered a new prayer book. I went to classes with women who prayed and prepared for the day when they might be ordained. Suddenly, I was engaged in the conflicts of the church again. Contrary to what I had known in the comparative liberality of a collegiate congregation, I discovered racist Episcopalians. I met conservative Anglo-Catholic Episcopalians and conservative Evangelical Episcopalians. I met Anglicans from other parts of the world. I met very wealthy Episcopalians and even very poor Episcopalians. I met gay and lesbian Episcopalians, and I met those whose opposition to homosexuality was a deeply held conviction. But I also noticed that these Christians seemed to tolerate this diversity; at their best, they even celebrated it.

But the times changed, and so did I. Things that had once challenged and invigorated me seemed more and more an intrusion and a headache. The Episcopal Church proved to be not very different from the Methodist Church. In fact, after a while, at certain levels, I came to see that it made little difference whether one was Episcopal, Methodist, Catholic, Jew, Hindu, or Muslim. At some levels, we are all very much alike. But we seem always to deny that similarity, or we lose it in the strife generated over our differences.

What I have related of my own experience seems less unique as I compare my story with others. Reading the Hebrew scriptures with a rabbi friend, I find the stories of our ancestors and their community strangely similar to my own. Pondering the Christian scriptures, and the history of the church that spawned them, I see more and more that is familiar. And I have learned that it is difficult to carry a two-edged sword without getting cut.

The crisis of difference posed in the first century by the conflict between Jewish and Gentile followers of Jesus was eventually resolved. Traditional Jews and the Christians—whether of Jewish or Gentile origin—parted company. Among Christians, issues of inclusion remained. In time the differences were sorted out and the community got on with its life. Regional differences in structure and worship continued to present flash points of conflict, and diverse theological perspectives challenged the collegiality of the whole.

From time to time it became necessary for representatives of the community to come together and confront the challenges. Just as they had gathered in Jerusalem to seek resolution on the matter of Gentile converts in what had up to that time been a predominantly Jewish community, so they gathered to confront and address other points of conflict.

By the middle of the second century, the four different accounts of the Gospel and thirteen of Paul's letters were widely accepted as the canon of Christian scripture—commonly called the New Testament. Within the following century, the Hebrew canon—commonly called the Old Testament—was similarly accepted as a legitimate part of the Christian scriptures. Again, this was a gradual process that involved several generations and much conflict.

The expansion of the church did a remarkable thing: it gathered diverse people into a common body. Christians are a people who have absolutely nothing in common, except Jesus. The experience of Jesus, like the person himself, crossed all boundaries. He was known and confessed by women, as well as men. According to some Gospel accounts, the first experiences of the living Jesus after his crucifixion were claimed by women. He crossed geographical boundaries. The book of the Acts of the Apostles and the epistles are vivid travelogues, introducing readers to various regions and practices. Christianity crossed political systems, surviving colonial rule, imperial wrath, and even imperial favor. It found root in monarchies, republics, democracies, dictatorships, and every other structure devised to order human affairs. Christ has been a vivid reality to slaves and to their owners, to prisoners and their captors.

So much diversity so impressed itself upon the church that the church eventually embraced diversity itself as a hallmark of its true identity. Creeds became necessary, not only to define the limits of universally accepted faith and doctrine, but also to affirm the very diversity that marked the institution. The Apostles' Creed, which may have been in common use by the fourth century, affirms the church as catholic. Likewise, the Nicene Creed, attributed to the fourth-century Council of Constantinople but certainly widely used by the fifth century, affirms the church as catholic. Embracing the diversity of universality is one thing, holding onto it is yet another. Even under the best of circumstances and in the very best of times, it has been difficult. More often than not it has been rather like gripping a tiger by the tail.

For a significant portion of contemporary Americans, memories of the church are steeped in images of stability. For that same generation, memories of the social and political order are associated with crisis. Two World Wars and the Great Depression preoccupied everyone's attention and demanded everyone's efforts. The role of the churches and the graceful message of the gospel in such times is understandably biased in favor of encouragement. Providing moral support, and in some cases literal sustenance through feeding, housing, clothing, medicine and education, the church is remembered, rightly, as a place of calm and order, of peace and prayer.

Lest we be too nostalgic, it is also true that even in such times, change does challenge the church. Churches were often the center of lively debate over whether and how the nation should be involved in those wars. They were frequently embroiled in labor conflicts. Even liturgy was a source of contention, as most any casual congregational "historian" reveals when the "war stories" are told of who left the church in a huff over the way a certain pastor prayed, a certain organist played, or a beloved memorial was, or was not, displayed.

To those who imagine the church a sanctuary in the midst of a rapidly changing world, the period since World War II has been most difficult. It has been a time of sustained economic growth. Recovering from war and domestic poverty, communities were reordered. Less and less are farms and factories the centers of common life and labor. We are more mobile and have greater choice over where we live and with whom we live.

The experience of World War II gave Americans a deep appreciation for military order and discipline. The influence of the military experience was so profound that it reshaped the way we live. By the end of the war, we were no longer forced by agriculture to live on isolated rural farms. We were no longer required by factories to live in crowded cities. We established suburban communities that were largely self-contained and, like military bases, stratified by rank. Until this time, we had hardly known a restricted neighborhood or building code, but very quickly we determined that all the houses in a subdivision would conform to certain standards— and so would the people within them. After the Depression's deprivations and war's threat, growing affluence and the sense of security it purchased gave the illusion of safe haven.

In a culture so ordered, the opposing edge of the gospel's sword challenged complacency and self-satisfaction. It challenged the inequities and the iniquities that accompanied growing affluence. Many churches became heavily involved in the African-American struggle for civil rights. The church felt the impact of an unpopular war in Vietnam and the growing disappointment in American government in the wake of Watergate. Americans were of many different minds on each of these issues, so it should have been no surprise that the churches soon were reeling as one blow after another struck.

The greatest "surprise" is that we should be surprised by all such conflict. Diversity is, after all, a virtue we have preached and long desired. It was differences—sometimes very profound and unresolvable differences—that propelled our ancestors to leave the relative security of families and homes for the perils of a transatlantic crossing to a wilderness. This nation was forged by conflict, and its political sovereignty was born out of revolution.

Tolerance of our differences frequently led to actual celebration of our diversity. We were proud to be a nation made of many nationalities. But something changed. There are probably many factors to which this change can be attributed, but the most neglected possibility is also the most difficult for Americans to accept: we may have reached our limit.

We are not a people to be easily restricted or restrained. The notion of limits is a challenge to our unbounded energy, optimism, and freedom. To confess to limitation is, in our minds, a confession of weakness. Confine us and we become anxious; limit us and we get angry. The very notion of limitation presents us with a challenge and constitutes a serious conflict.

In my recollections of college, I wrote of the tremendous changes demanded of me. As a university chaplain, I work with students. And we still demand significant changes when they arrive on campus. We uproot them from family and friends and place them in a dorm room with a complete stranger. That stranger may be of a different race or nationality, or of a different sexuality. That stranger will certainly have different habits and preferences. We place them on the same hall with other strangers, who are also of different races and nationalities, and of different gender—since many dorms are now coed. On our particular campus, we place these dorms in the midst of a multiracial urban neighborhood, so negotiating the simple tasks of shopping and eating and traveling necessitates interaction with yet more strangers.

Such adaptation is a great deal to ask of a person, but we make it even more difficult. For now, in the interest of civility, we demand that all the frustration and anxiety of such change be tempered by thoughtful politeness. Anger and frustration must be ordered for the sake of community. It is truly a marvel that we do as well as we do. When things do break down, when the anger and frustration can no longer be contained, the resulting conflict is quite understandable.

There are limits on how much any of us can be pressed to process. At present, those limits are being assaulted by the overwhelming barrage of information we are asked to process every day. I might temper this point by noting that we ourselves allow these intrusions. No one forces me to have a telephone, or to answer it. No one forces me to own a television, or to watch it. No one demands that I have a radio, or listen to it. But I do have a telephone—several, in fact: one line at home, two lines into my office. And I have answering machines at home and in the office. I also have mailboxes—the regular kind and an electronic "mailbox" accessed through my computer. I have two televisions, one in the kitchen and one in my den. I have radios at home, in my office, and in my car.

I am very much in touch with the world, or a large chunk of it, and it is very much in touch with me. More and more, I am introduced to the diversity of the world. I am exposed to more information than I could ever use, more questions than could ever be answered. I am challenged to consider heartbreaking problems for which neither I nor anyone else has an answer, or sympathy to embrace. I am made mindful of more danger than any nervous system can bear, and the graphic depiction of more evil than even Satan on the most creative day could imagine. I am offered more goods than I could ever consume, and yet I am given less constructive help than I need to end each day in peace.

Jesus calls us to be in the world, but not of the world. But just being in the world nowadays is sufficient to break the best of us. Therefore, I find it quite understandable that we are in retreat, even if we call it something else. Our tendency to isolate ourselves, to spend more time alone, is an antidote to the daily crush. But so is our tendency to limit our concern, to place our selves and our families first, and to give less attention to those beyond. Our national impulse to shy from involvement in expansive and expensive government programs is a logical response to the endless demands placed upon us and our resources. We are not necessarily more selfish, even though it often looks that way. We *are* more aware of our limitations, though we deny and mask our awareness behind a false bravado. When all is said and done, we would rather be accounted selfish than weak.

Our predicament is compounded by the changing shape of governance in our lives. After decades of representative government, we have been disappointed with the results. Elected leaders have so frustrated us that we have grown cynical. Participation in elections dwindles with each political campaign. Our ambivalence is painfully evident in our willingness to elect to office those who promise us a change from what we have known, then refuse to make the changes they demand of us.

We are only beginning to make the transition to the participatory government envisioned in the American experiment (for it is an experiment still in process). This, too, is a change we greet warily. We want the authority to make decisions, but we do not want the responsibility that accompanies that authority. For the first two hundred years of our life together as a nation, we entrusted most of the authority and responsibility to an elite corps of politicians. Now we want some of that authority back. Just how authority should be exercised and by whom, as well as just what responsibilities ensue and who is accountable, are issues with which we struggle in the political arena.

But is this not also true in the personal and the religious arenas? Dependence on male authority and responsibility in households, and in the workplace, is challenged by reallocation of authority and responsibility to women. The hegemony of white male leadership has given way to greater diversity. These changes are sometimes dictated literally by those who wield the powers of persuasion. But more and more, they are demanded by circumstance as the accustomed patterns of family and the work force change.

In the church we face a crisis of leadership. It is not that we have too few leaders, or even leaders of insufficient quality. On the contrary, we have an abundance of leaders and many of high quality, but they have for many years abdicated their prerogative to lead. They appointed an elite clergy to bear authority and responsibility in far too great measure.

The transition to greater lay leadership in the church is itself a source of considerable conflict. Clergy are challenged to share authority and responsibility, but may not have been prepared for this mutual ministry. The suggestion that ministry can be shared is greeted not as an opportunity, but as a judgment on their ability. Yet something similar can be said of the lay person who is challenged to accept authority and responsibility, but finds such a suggestion not an encouragement but an imposition.

These changes demanded of the reapportionment of authority and responsibility also have their analogy on campus. In the classroom, students' preconceived notions of the world are challenged, and they are encouraged to imagine new possibilities. What they have learned is called into question, and they are invited to explore every facet anew. The point is not that what they have previously learned is wrong or false. It is that they must learn the authority of their own experience and weigh their own perceptions of truth.

The university does not challenge students in order to destroy them, but to strengthen them. It is like the difference between watching a football game and playing a football game. While there is a certain amount of enjoyment in watching a player's firsthand experience of the game, one can become a player only by experiencing the grueling practice exercises and actually working with others on the playing field. Neither life nor a living faith is a spectator sport. But getting the fans out of the bleachers and onto the field is hard business. And making the transition—from a world where some sit and watch, while others exercise the authority and bear the responsibility, to a world where everyone contributes to the whole—goes against the prevailing tide of human nature and human affairs. Jesus found that to be true, and so will those who follow him.

Our crisis is exacerbated by time. The wages of sin may be death, but those wages are calculated in time. There are only so many hours in a day, and only so many years in a lifetime. Death is the limit of a lifetime and, as such, is a formidable force. Even if I had the *ability* to process all the changes demanded of me, would I have the *time*?

The instruments that challenge me daily with the intrusive news of the world's diversity—telephones, televisions, and all related technologies—challenge my notion of time. It took my Sicilian grandparents eight days or more to cross the Atlantic under steam; I can do it in about eight hours by air, and fewer if I take the Concorde. I can carry on a conversation with my Sicilian cousins by phone. News of Africa, complete with pictures, will be beamed live into my kitchen while I am preparing dinner tonight. I transmitted a note to a friend in Hong Kong over electronic mail; within seconds he answered it.

It is not our imagination. The world really is moving faster, because we are moving faster. And our minds and emotions are moving faster. The speed is dizzying, and if we occasionally skid on an intellectual curve or get a painful case of emotional whiplash, that is the price of our acceleration. As time picks up its pace, we become more mindful of our mortality and its nearness. This is a natural consequence of aging. But why does it seem conversely (and perversely) true that as our actual lifespan has increased, time itself has diminished?

The crisis today cannot be narrowed to any single issue. Our crisis is no one thing; it is everything, all at once. Our crisis is created by seemingly endless demands, made by a growing number of challenges, confronted in an increased diversity, crowded into diminishing time and space. Our crisis is that we are up against our limits. And like any captive, caged animal, we lash back. We strike out at the cage, at the invisible captor. In our panic, we strike each other, wounding those who are caught in the cage with us. We tear at the limits, clawing at the restraints, and sometimes we do painful damage to ourselves.

Yet, we are where we are not because of failure, but because of success. In the Church, we are beset by challenges because we have baptized and received into community a breathtaking variety of people. We are women and men, young and old. We are Catholic, Evangelical, Protestant, Pentecostal and Charismatic. We are married, single, divorced and celibate. We are heterosexual, homosexual, bisexual and asexual. We are of many races and ethnic ancestries.

Consider the anomaly of the Episcopal Church. We are members of the Anglican Communion, a worldwide federation of congregations whose English name stands in blatant contrast to its myriad hues of skin and multitude of languages. The Anglican Communion, whose name is the very epitome of white, Western European, hegemony, is one of the largest Black communities of Christians in the world. In my own diocese, a liturgy steeped in the literary tradition of Britain is heard increasingly in Spanish and Korean. The Episcopal name, signifying the leadership of bishops, more and more identifies a church governed by its lay members. It is all very strange, very different, very confusing, and very challenging.

We are anxious. We are frightened, angry, frustrated, and in distress. And we are the ones who have been commissioned to share the gospel with the world! We are hemmed in on every side. We are hard-pressed. We are, ironically and providentially, ideally poised to hear the gospel.

Chapter 7
Blessed Conflict

THIS BOOK BEGAN WITH THE ASSERTION THAT CHURCH AND SOCI-
ETY ARE IN CRISIS. Its central thesis and substance is that the
church has, since its beginning, been in crisis. It should
be no surprise, then, that this book comes full circle to the conclusion that the church remains in crisis.

Some will be disappointed by this outcome. Certainly, anyone seeking a specific answer to the unsettling questions that
bedevil us or a neat resolution to the conflicts that mark our life
will find little comfort here.

But crisis and conflict are not fatal. This much is abundantly clear from the testimonies of generations of believers who
claim the inheritance of Jesus. Regardless of what one believes
of the resurrection of Jesus, the inherent message of that resurrection is that nothing—not even crisis and conflict—can ever
separate us from the life and love of God.

How, then, are we to see these forces of conflict and crisis?
Perhaps more immediately, how are we to live with them? I
have attempted to show that difference is an inherent characteristic of a genuinely creative God, and that conflict is the
inevitable result of difference meeting difference. Conflict is the
logical outcome of life in any place or time that welcomes the
diversity of God's creativity. Therefore, we find ourselves in
conflict not because we have done something "wrong," or
because we have "sinned," but for the opposite reasons. We
find ourselves in conflict because we have more nearly approx-
imated the inclusive embrace of a God who delights in our differences. We find ourselves in conflict not because we have
sinned, but because we have attempted genuine righteousness,
because we are seeking wholeness—a wholeness that honors
the fullness of God's creativity.

Conflict is not undesirable. It is of the very essence of life
within a community that values difference and honors the

diversity of God's creative design evidenced in humanity. Conflict certainly has destructive, or demonic, possibilities in its ability to drive us apart and keep us separate from one another. But conflict is also the outward and visible sign of the perpetual work of the church, the work of identifying, proclaiming, nurturing, and celebrating the community God has given us in each other. Conflict is to the body of Christ, the church, what breath is to the human body. The evidence of conflict, like the light vapor that clouds the mirror held to the dying person's lips, is sometimes the only sign we have to reassure us of life in this body that has in many generations been pronounced dead.

Crisis, too, is vital to the church. Crisis is a mark of our life. *Crisis* means, literally, "decision." For the Christian, crisis is the dynamic of the faithful life. If conflict is the breath of the church, crisis is its heartbeat.

To "decide for Christ" is a crucial turning point in anyone's life. But deciding for Christ is not a single, discrete act. It may be a very memorable and dramatic act; it may be a very distinctive act. But it is never a final act. A wedding is a distinct, memorable, and dramatic act. But the wedding is only the prelude to marriage. Marriage is the daily reenactment of the wedding, the daily renewal of the vow to love one's partner unreservedly and unconditionally.

Crisis is the daily reaffirmation of the baptismal promise to love God in Christ Jesus, in all the many manifestations that touch our human experience. Every moment provides a new occasion to "decide for Christ." And conflict is often the arena that most challenges us, because conflict presents us with many demands and opportunities to decide.

The particular crises confronting the church as I write these words seem all-consuming. The particular crisis of Gentile inclusion in the early Jewish community that confessed faith in Jesus dominated its life and letters in its first century. It is noteworthy that this single "domestic" concern of the institution dominates the documents preserved from that period, many of which form the heart of our scriptural canon.

There were other concerns in that first century, some far more dramatic and dangerous than the Gentile controversy. Believers in that time suffered grave persecution and martyrdom, yet few references to either are found in our texts. We know precious little about the circle of friends who gathered around Jesus in his own lifetime as they presumably went about their lives after his death.

The Gentile controversy, important as it was at the time (and as helpful as it has been in working through similar issues in our life together), could not have been the most salient issue for the early church. Yet it seems at times to have overshadowed any and every other consideration. Perhaps the same will be true for those who look back to our own time in search of precedents. They will find, as we do, that the controversies are neither as interesting nor as important as the processes and the principles by which they are decided.

Those issues that preoccupy us today are many and diverse, but they are also temporal and, thus, temporary. Were we to "resolve" them all tomorrow, the day after would present us with a fresh set of problems. There remains, however, a distinctly universal crisis for the Christian believer. In every time and place, each of us in every moment is presented with the opportunity and challenged by the demand to decide. The church is now and always has been in crisis, and the crisis that drives our life is the crisis of the three cardinal virtues: the crises of faith, hope, and love.

In all conflicts that touch our individual lives and our life together, the fundamental crises are the same—for they challenge our faith, our hope, and our love. It makes no difference where one finds oneself on the political spectrum, whether at the liberal extreme, the conservative extreme, or anywhere along the road between, the basic questions to decide are questions of faith, hope, and love.

In any given moment, I am called upon to decide what I shall believe of God. But I am also called to decide what I shall believe of my neighbor—humankind in its particular and general manifestations—and I am called to decide what I shall believe of myself. Similarly, my hope in God, neighbor, and self hangs in the balance. Finally, love of God, neighbor, and self must be negotiated and articulated in action. What I believe will determine the response I make. And, most significant for the Christian, the response I make will be my most vivid witness to the world.

It is this matter of witness that is the most important concern for the church in crisis. The point is not that we should be over-concerned with appearances, but that our actions will always speak and be interpreted more profoundly than our words. This extends not only to the words of our discourse, but to the words of our written documents and pronouncements, as well.

Consider again the marriage analogy. One can loudly and effusively express affection for one's partner in the company of friends and colleagues, but from a single sharp word to that partner within public earshot, all will form their own assessments of the quality of love in the relationship. Those assessments may not take into account the exceptional nature of one angry word in a lifetime of commitment, the circumstantial nature of such anger, or the appropriateness of that anger as answer to certain provocation, but none of that matters. What matters is the dissonance between the love confessed and the lack of love displayed.

The common response to conflict, both in the church and outside the church, reveals neither faith, nor hope, nor love. The most pronounced witness in our midst is a witness to fear.

The opponent of faith is not doubt, but fear. Yet faith is far more than a denial or dismissal of fear. As is true of so many paradoxes, fear and faith are in perpetual tension, or conflict, with each other. As Christians, we affirm that new life proceeds out of death. This profession of received truth does little to encourage our embrace of death. We are as reluctant as any to live into death. Similarly, while we may readily affirm that faith is the antidote to fear, we are hardly encouraged by that confession to embrace fear enthusiastically.

Fear is a legitimate human emotion. Like death and the threat of death, fear is widely considered a negative dimension of life, something to be avoided. Only the saint or the person ravaged in mind or body embraces death in welcome. Likewise, it is the rare person, indeed, who can find strength in fear.

Conflict is frightening. It threatens our sense of control and upsets our notions of order. It touches our vulnerability and reveals uncomfortable realities. Therefore, we tend to deny conflict, or we try to manage it, tame it. In fantasies of ultimate

control, we banish conflict altogether. In my fantasies of ultimate control—which is to say, in my own fantasies of the
Original Sin wherein I get to be God—there is no conflict. In
those fantasies there is no conflict, because everyone is in agreement with me. The world and everything in it is ordered to my
liking, according to my design.

But the ways of God in the real and quite tangible world in
which I live are obviously not the same as my ways. In this
world, I am rarely in agreement with others and God obviously tolerates much more untidiness than I find comfortable. This
conflict, which is with me every hour and becomes quite apparent hundreds of times a day, arouses fear within me. I want to
be in control, and yet I cannot be in control.

In the crisis of this conflict, I am called upon to decide. What
shall I believe? Do I believe that God is ultimately in control?
Can I relinquish my own desire to control and be confident
that God will remain in control, that God will bring God's own
order out of the chaos around me? Do I have sufficient faith in
God to let go?

Do I have sufficient faith in my neighbor to let go? Can I
trust my neighbor in chaos? Can I trust God's relationship with
my neighbor, and my neighbor's relationship with God, to prevail in the chaos of conflict? Can I give myself over to others, to
their processes and actions, even when I fear that those designs
are destructive? Can I trust others when my own life—everything that I deem precious, either figuratively or literally, or
both—hangs in the balance?

Do I have sufficient faith in myself to let go? Can I give
myself up? Do I even have sufficient possession of myself to
offer myself willingly to the conflict and the God in the midst
of that conflict? Do I have sufficient faith in God's affirmation
of me, of God's claims upon me, to let go?

And what of my hope? Hope in its most literal sense is
desire of fulfillment. Do I really want God's will to be fulfilled?
Do I truly want the fulfillment of my neighbor's life? Do I genuinely desire the fulfillment of my own life?

Or am I holding back? Do I desire that God's fulfillment be
given precedence over my own? Can I desire my neighbor's fulfillment when I fear my own diminishment? Do I truly desire

the fulfillment of my life—which is utterly beyond my imagining—over the safety of what I can know and the security of my own control?

And what of love? Do I love God, or am I only infatuated with my own notion of God? Do I love—can I love—a God who looks and acts like my neighbor, a God who is incarnate in the perplexing and demanding diversity of my neighbor? Can I love a God who relates to the world from the perspective of a different gender or sexuality or race, a God who speaks a different language, is loyal to a different political order? Do I love—can I love—a God who made me, who loves me more profoundly and more passionately than I can love myself?

These questions and their thousands are raised simultaneously in every moment for the Christian. They are processed with a speed more dizzying than that of any computer. The outcome is our witness, it is what the world sees—a window into what we are made of.

Christian witness is made of word and deed. When word and deed meet in true congruence, we are given a glimpse into God's reality. Throughout this book, I have drawn upon certain experiences that opened windows into the stories of scripture. In those experiences I saw, or came to see, the happy convergence of words I had read, or heard, or even spoken, and concrete actions that made those words come to life in a new way. These experiences became stories, ways of speaking about life and ways of speaking about God, neighbor, and self.

As I come to the end of this book, I see most prominently the words *conflict, crisis,* and *fear.* None of these words is associated in common human experience with anything approximating a "happy ending." Paradoxically, the story out of my own experience that wants most to be told is a story that I associate with conflict, crisis, and fear. It seems an apt and adequate parable of our present predicaments and our perpetual task.

The setting of my story is a national conference. Those present represented the diversity of the Episcopal Church. As the conference progressed, it was plainly evident in the conversations and arguments that were shared and/or overheard that we had come from many perspectives and were not of a single mind.

I had been asked by the conference leadership to be responsible for a workshop on homosexuality and the church. I agreed to the assignment, but really did not know what I would do in the time allotted. Having participated in several national, diocesan, and parish groups and commissions charged with studying this issue, I knew that I did not want to pursue a path that quickly divided people into adversarial argumentation. Yet, I had no idea how to accomplish this.

As time for the workshop drew near, my anxiety increased. When the hour arrived and I reported to the assigned meeting room, I was surprised to see about forty people present. I was even more surprised to see that in addition to the few people I expected to see—those who had openly revealed their homosexuality and had expressed interest in talking about it in nearly every forum on nearly every occasion—there were others present. There were some who clutched well-worn Bibles, who had been ardent in their confession of literal scriptural interpretation. And there were others less easily identified or categorized.

Just as I had no idea of what I would do, I had even less notion of where this exploration would go. In short, I and the situation for which I was responsible were out of control. I was afraid.

Then I took a deep breath. I suggested we begin in the usual fashion by introducing ourselves and indicating why each of us had come to the workshop. At the very least, I thought, this would give me time to figure out what to do next.

The diversity I had only superficially noted in the group began to grow in depth and breadth as each person spoke. We were from all over the country. We were of different ages and races. We were of diverse theological traditions, even though we shared the same communion. We were of quite different experiences.

Some were present because they were, indeed, homosexual and took a personal interest in such discussions, anxious to defend their sexuality and themselves. Some had friends or family members who were homosexual. Some admitted that they had much difficulty with the issue of homosexuality and wanted to present what they believed to be a biblically based rejoinder to liberal ideology.

As I listened to these disclosures, my anxiety grew. Helpful as our opening exercise had been, it still did not move us beyond the level of preliminary sparring, the tentative posturing boxers use to assess each other in the opening moments of a match. My anxieties were not relieved. I was still afraid.

When we had gone full circle and it was my turn again, I confessed my fear. I told the group that I had come to the workshop with anxiety and that I continued to be fearful. I tried to articulate those fears as best I could—fear of conflict, fear of failure. In acknowledging my own fear, I found that the group seemed quite understanding. I realized that, for many good reasons, the subject of the workshop was frightening. It occurred to me that while we were very different in our experience with the subject of homosexuality, we did hold two things in common. We were united by a common baptism. And we were united in fear.

I suggested that we go around the circle again. This time, we would tell of our fears. We would acknowledge and even honor the fears. The journey around the circle was transforming. Each person was able to articulate his or her fear quite specifically, revealing that each of us had obviously spent time in close communion with that fear. Even more interestingly, while some had found commonality in their introductions—several were from the same state or town or school, several had come to the workshop for the same reason—no two person's fears were alike. We were even more diverse in our fear than in our faith.

One person's story was particularly moving. He told of his friendship with a high school classmate. The two boys had been very close for many years. But when his friend disclosed his homosexuality, it touched the fears of this member of our group. He felt helpless to respond to his friend, for he was immobilized by his own fear. Afraid of what his peers would think of him for his relationship with an avowed homosexual, he was at even greater pains to distance himself. When his friend was rejected by family, he could not bring himself to extend a helping hand. When his friend committed suicide, this person realized the power of his own fear, and its cost. He had come to our conversation resolved to face his fear so that this might never happen again.

Others told their own stories of fear. Gay men and lesbian women shared their fear of rejection and loss—afraid of losing family and friends, and the love of God and God's church. Each story possessed specifics as distinct as the physical characteristics that made each person unique.

I was particularly struck by one person who professed a conservative fundamentalism and sat with Bible in hand but confessed, "I am here to listen and to learn, for I fear that in my zeal or ignorance, I may bring great harm to a brother or sister in Christ who is homosexual." It was a breathtaking moment; this certainly was unlike any conversation on homosexuality I had ever experienced. The circuit was completed a second time. There was one thing more to be done. Once again I ventured a suggestion.

Among most modern people, even confessing Christians, conversation on personal faith is a fearful thing. Many "mainline" Christians are uncomfortable with personal witness, fearful that any personal revelation will expose them to ridicule or scorn. Even aggressive Evangelical Christians seem more preoccupied with the salvation of others than comfortable with personal story. Their outreach is often cast in formulaic speeches liberally laced with the jargon of their Christian subculture. The same is true of devout "catholic" or high-church Christians, who can discourse for hours on the merits of eucharistic fellowship, private devotion, and sacramental confession, but blanch at the thought of personalizing their experience of God.

Still, the workshop group had begun the process of building relationship with one another, and the ease with which each one personalized his or her experience encouraged me to pursue what I can only now describe as "intimations of the Spirit." We would go around the circle one more time. This time, each was invited to share a single, simple story. Please share with us, I asked, a moment when you genuinely felt—when you knew— you met the Christ.

The allotted time for the workshop expired, and only half of those present had told their stories. I was committed to move to a second group and commence a workshop on an entirely different subject. I asked for the mind of the group. They decided that they would remain and continue their dialogue. Though I had entered the room in fear, I departed refreshed, renewed, and with a sure and certain knowledge that I had truly met the Christ.

The group continued, I was later told, until each had had an opportunity to share, to witness. Each had done what Christians have for centuries done—they told one another of the marvelous works of God in their lives. Were we faithful to the task? Yes, I believe we were. We did have a conversation on homosexuality, one of the best and most productive I have ever experienced. Yet we did not dwell on anatomical or biological detail. We did not engage theological, political, or social controversy. We began with the only two things we had in common, Jesus and fear, and we became the church at Pentecost all over again. Each of us came from different places, varied experiences, even speaking different languages. Yet, when we shared our fears and told of the marvelous works of God in our lives, we found a new understanding of one another. We enjoyed a genuine comprehension, the expansive embrace of God that held us in love and care.

Conflict, crisis, fear. They have been, they are, and they likely shall be with us always. Like everything in God's creation entrusted to freedom, they hold potential for evil. But they also hold potential for good. Like everything God has made, they are redeemed and made whole in Christ. They are gifts.

And we are stewards of these gifts. What, then, shall we do? Shall we deny these gifts, or spurn them? Shall we use these gifts to our own selfish ends, as the means for gaining power or advantage over others? Shall we submit to their tyranny, bowing down before them in subjection? Or shall we accept them with gratitude, honor and respect them, share and confess them? Shall we let God work in and through them to turn us around, to reorient us?

Blessed conflict, happy revolution, that turns us toward one another and brings us face to face with God.